Non-verbal Reasoning

Assessment Papers

Up to Speed

9–10 years

Great Clarendon Street, Oxford, OX2 6DP, United Kingdom

Oxford University Press is a department of the University of Oxford. It furthers the University's objective of excellence in research, scholarship, and education by publishing worldwide. Oxford is a registered trade mark of Oxford University Press in the UK and in certain other countries

Text © Alison Primrose 2015
Illustrations © Oxford University Press 2015

The moral rights of the authors have been asserted

First published in 2015
This edition published in 2022

All rights reserved. No part of this publication may be reproduced, stored in a retrieval system, or transmitted, in any form or by any means, without the prior permission in writing of Oxford University Press, or as expressly permitted by law, by licence or under terms agreed with the appropriate reprographics rights organization. Enquiries concerning reproduction outside the scope of the above should be sent to the Rights Department, Oxford University Press, at the address above.

You must not circulate this work in any other form and you must impose this same condition on any acquirer

British Library Cataloguing in Publication Data
Data available

978-0-19-278513-8

10 9 8 7 6 5 4 3 2

Paper used in the production of this book is a natural, recyclable product made from wood grown in sustainable forests.
The manufacturing process conforms to the environmental regulations of the country of origin.

Printed in Great Britain by Ashford Colour Press Ltd

Acknowledgements

The publishers would like to thank the following for permissions to use copyright material:

Page make-up: eMC Design Ltd
Illustrations: OKS Prepress, India
Cover illustrations: Lo Cole

Although we have made every effort to trace and contact all copyright holders before publication this has not been possible in all cases. If notified, the publisher will rectify any errors or omissions at the earliest opportunity.

Links to third party websites are provided by Oxford in good faith and for information only. Oxford disclaims any responsibility for the materials contained in any third party website referenced in this work.

What is Bond?

The Bond *Up to Speed* titles are part of the Bond range of assessment papers, the number one series for the 11+, selective exams and general practice. Bond *Up to Speed* is carefully designed to support children who need less challenging activities than those in the regular age-appropriate Bond papers, in order to build up and improve their techniques and confidence.

How does this book work?

The book contains two distinct sets of papers, along with full answers and a Progress Chart.

- Focus tests, accompanied by advice and directions, are focused on particular (and age-appropriate) non-verbal reasoning question types encountered in the 11+ and other exams. The questions are deliberately set at a less challenging level than the standard *Assessment Papers*. Each Focus test is designed to help a child 'catch' their level in a particular question type, and then gently raise it through the course of the test and the subsequent Mixed papers.

- Mixed papers are longer tests containing a full range of non-verbal reasoning question types. These are designed to provide rigorous practice with less challenging questions, perhaps against the clock, in order to help children acquire and develop the necessary skills and techniques for 11+ success.

Full answers are provided for both types of test in the middle of the book.

How much time should the tests take?

The tests are for practice and to reinforce learning, and you may wish to test exam techniques and working to a set time limit. Using the Mixed papers, we would recommend that your child spends 25 minutes answering the 36 questions in each paper.

You can reduce the suggested time by 5 minutes to practise working at speed.

Using the Progress Chart

The Progress Chart can be used to track Focus test and Mixed paper results over time to monitor how well your child is doing and identify any repeated problems in tackling the different question types.

Focus test 1 — Similarities

In these questions, you must identify the features that all the shapes have in common to find the correct answer. In some questions there are two options for one feature, so the correct answer may contain either one of these features.

Which one belongs to the group on the left? Circle the letter.

Example

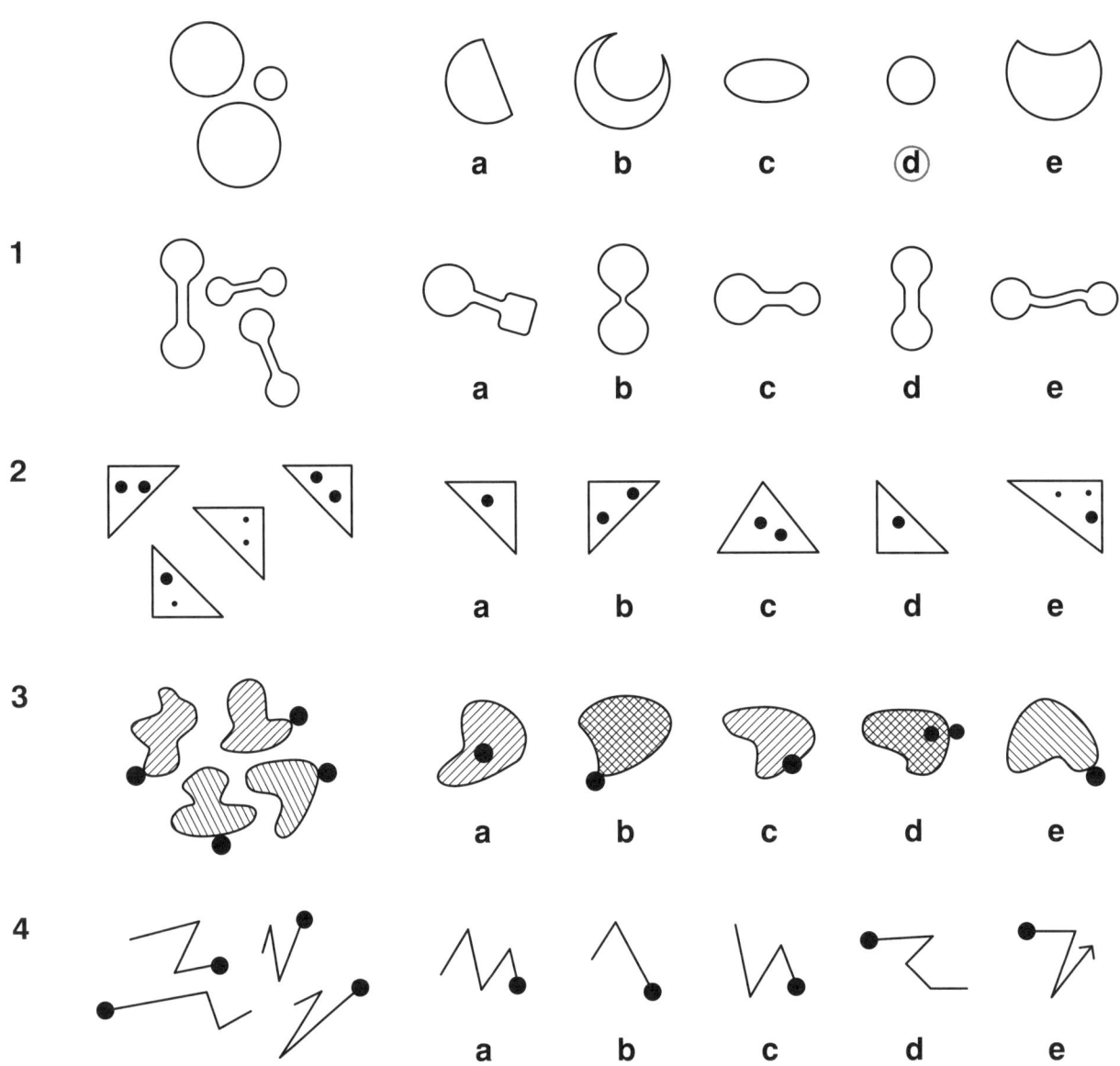

5

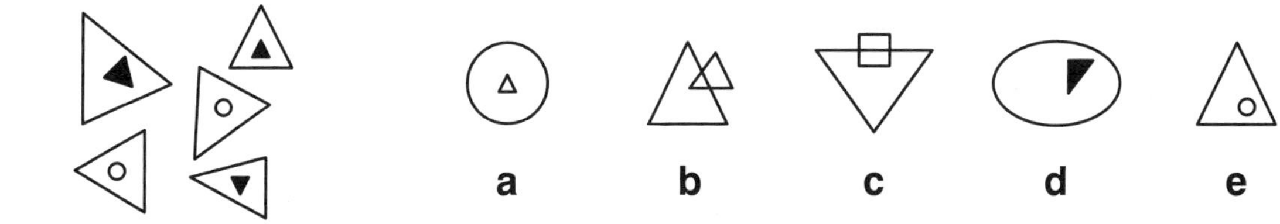

6

7

8

9

10

Try it yourself ...
Draw a group of shapes to which answer option 'c' would belong, but not the others, and then test a friend.

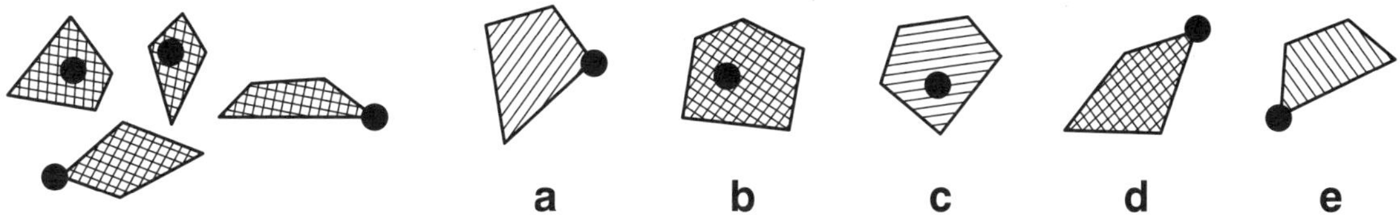

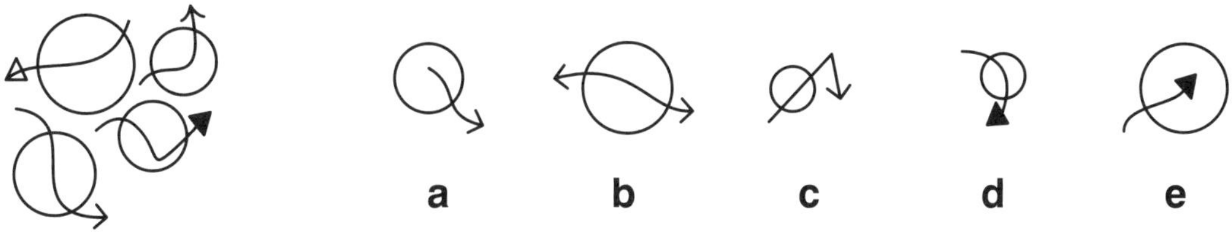

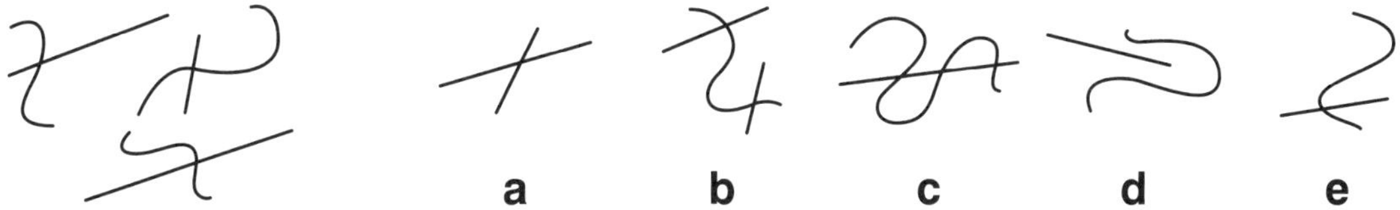

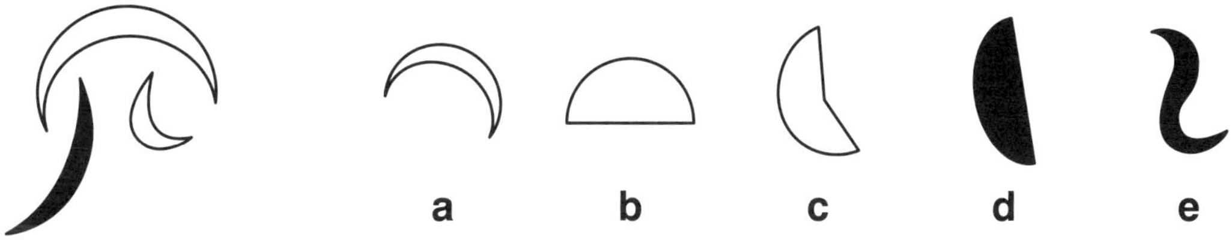

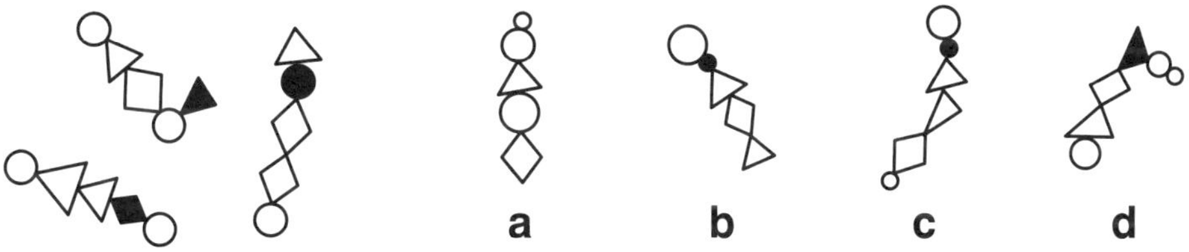

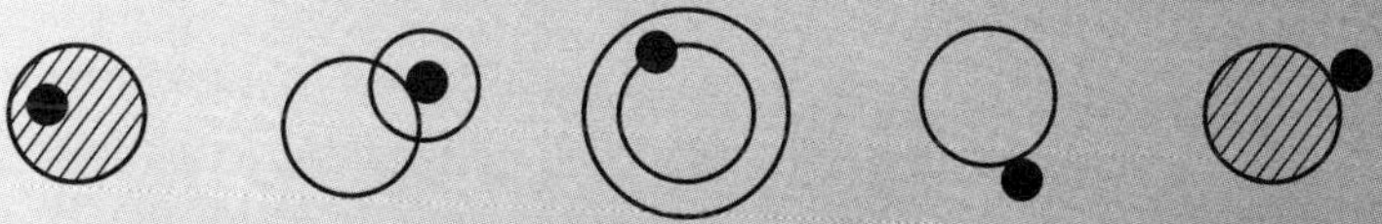

Now go to the Progress Chart ... 5 *... to record your score!* Total 10

Focus test 2 — Analogies

Look carefully at the first two pictures. You need to find the connection or link between them. How have parts of the first picture been changed in the second one? Once you have seen the connection or link, you must apply it to the third picture to work out which answer option completes the second pair in the same way as the first pair. Often, more than one part is changed!

Which one completes the second pair in the same way as the first pair? Circle the letter.

Example

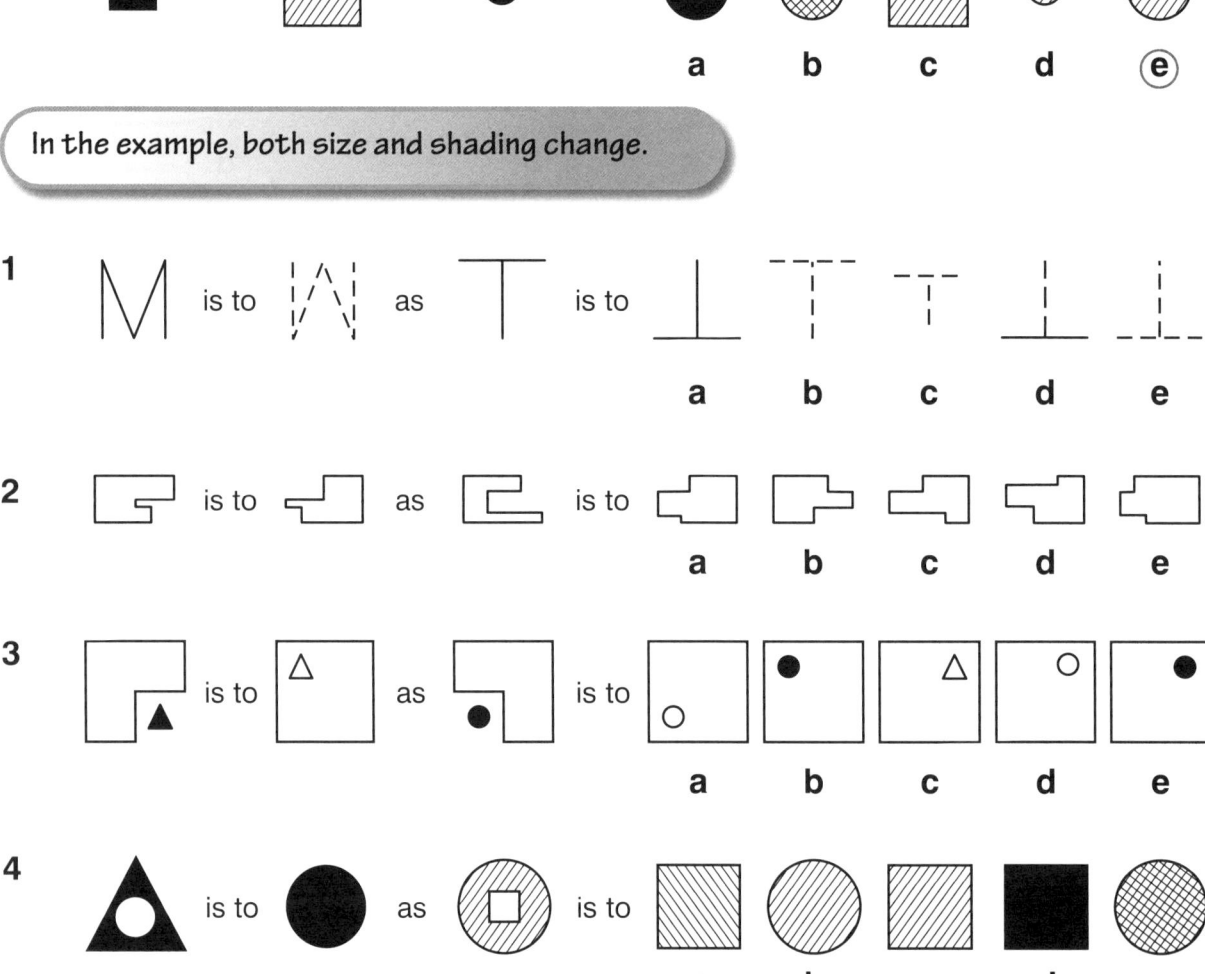

In the example, both size and shading change.

5

> The connection between the first two pictures may be a reflection or a rotation. When choosing the picture to complete the second pair, look very carefully at lines and angles.

6

7

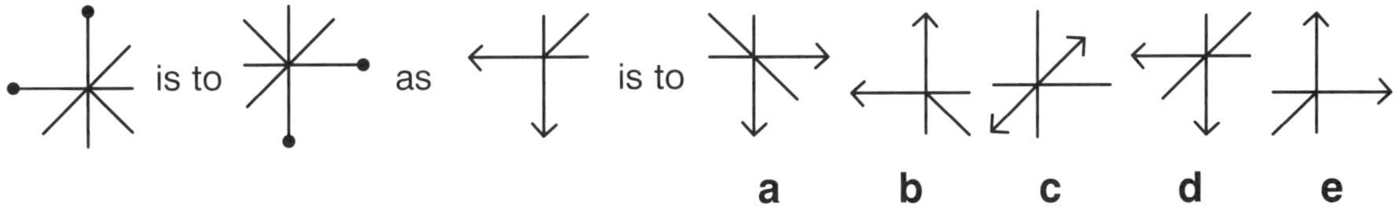

8

9

10

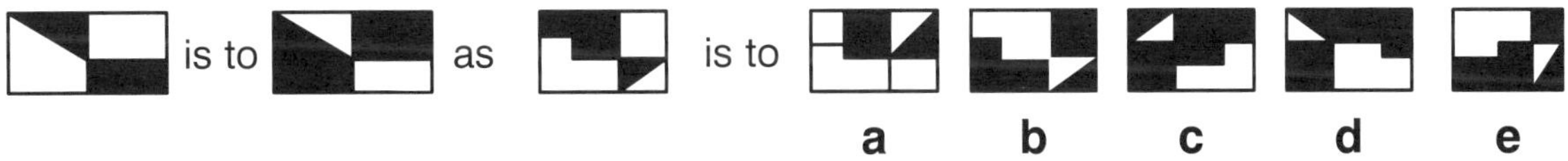

Try it yourself …
See if you can make up a second part to this analogy question. Give five answer choices and then test a friend!

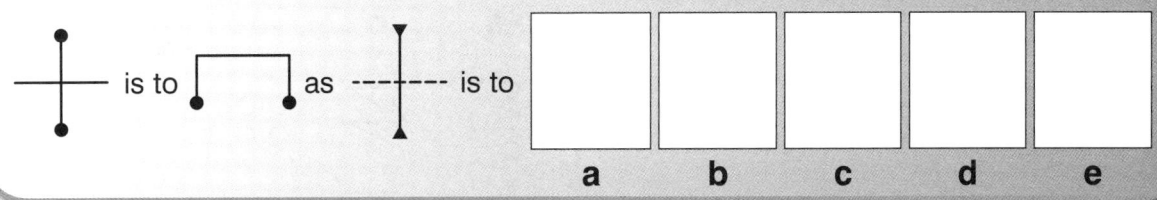

Now go to the Progress Chart … 7 … to record your score! Total 10

Focus test 3 — Sequences

To find the pattern that continues or completes a sequence, look carefully at the changes at each step. More than one feature may change. If the missing pattern is partway through the sequence, check your answer choice by working back from the end as well as the beginning.

Which one completes the sequence? Circle the letter.

Example

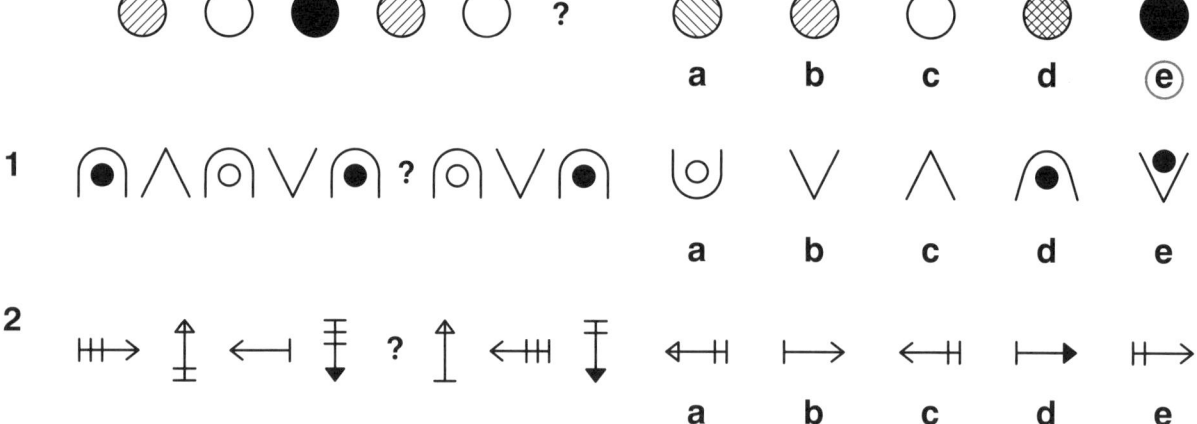

In the next question it is not clear what the missing pattern will be, so you need to choose the most logical and sensible of the options.

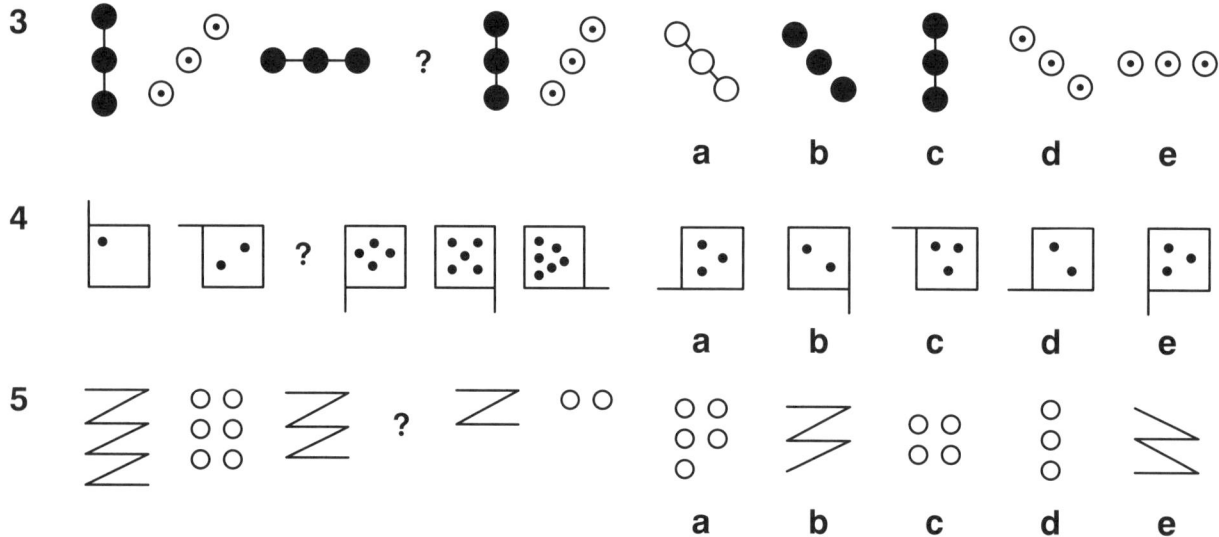

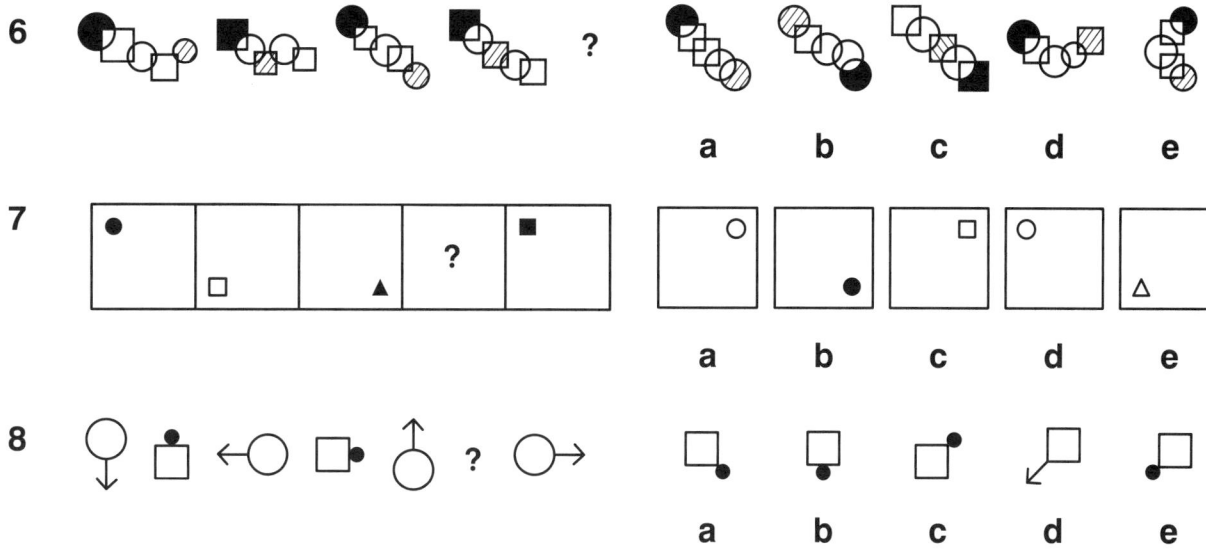

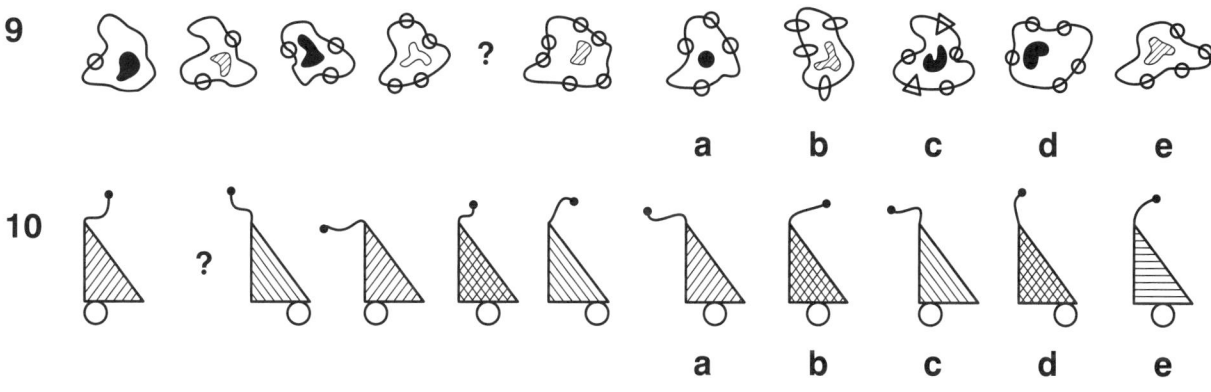

Some sequences include features that are not part of the sequence! The next two questions have extra features – see if you can identify them, then ignore them as they do not help you find the answer.

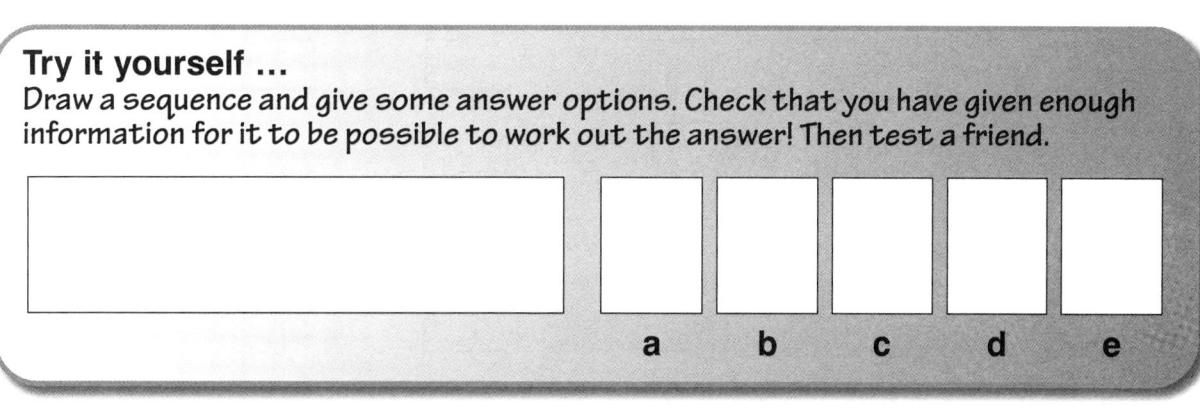

Try it yourself …
Draw a sequence and give some answer options. Check that you have given enough information for it to be possible to work out the answer! Then test a friend.

a   b   c   d   e

Focus test 4 — Reflections

In these questions, you have to find the reflection, or mirror image, of a pattern. Look carefully at every detail – especially the direction of any shading lines, as these must also be reflected.

Which one is a reflection of the pattern on the left? Circle the letter.

Example

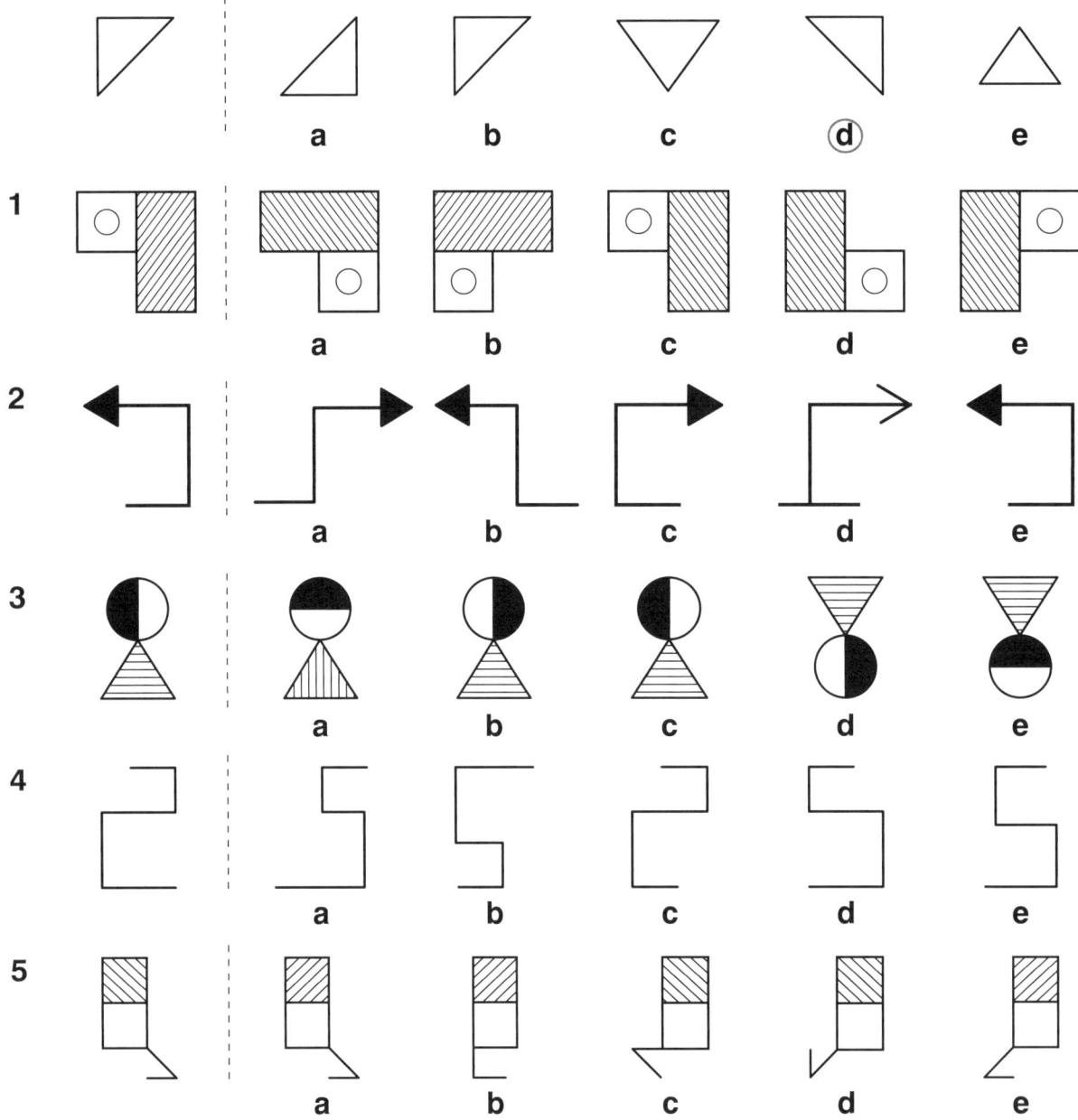

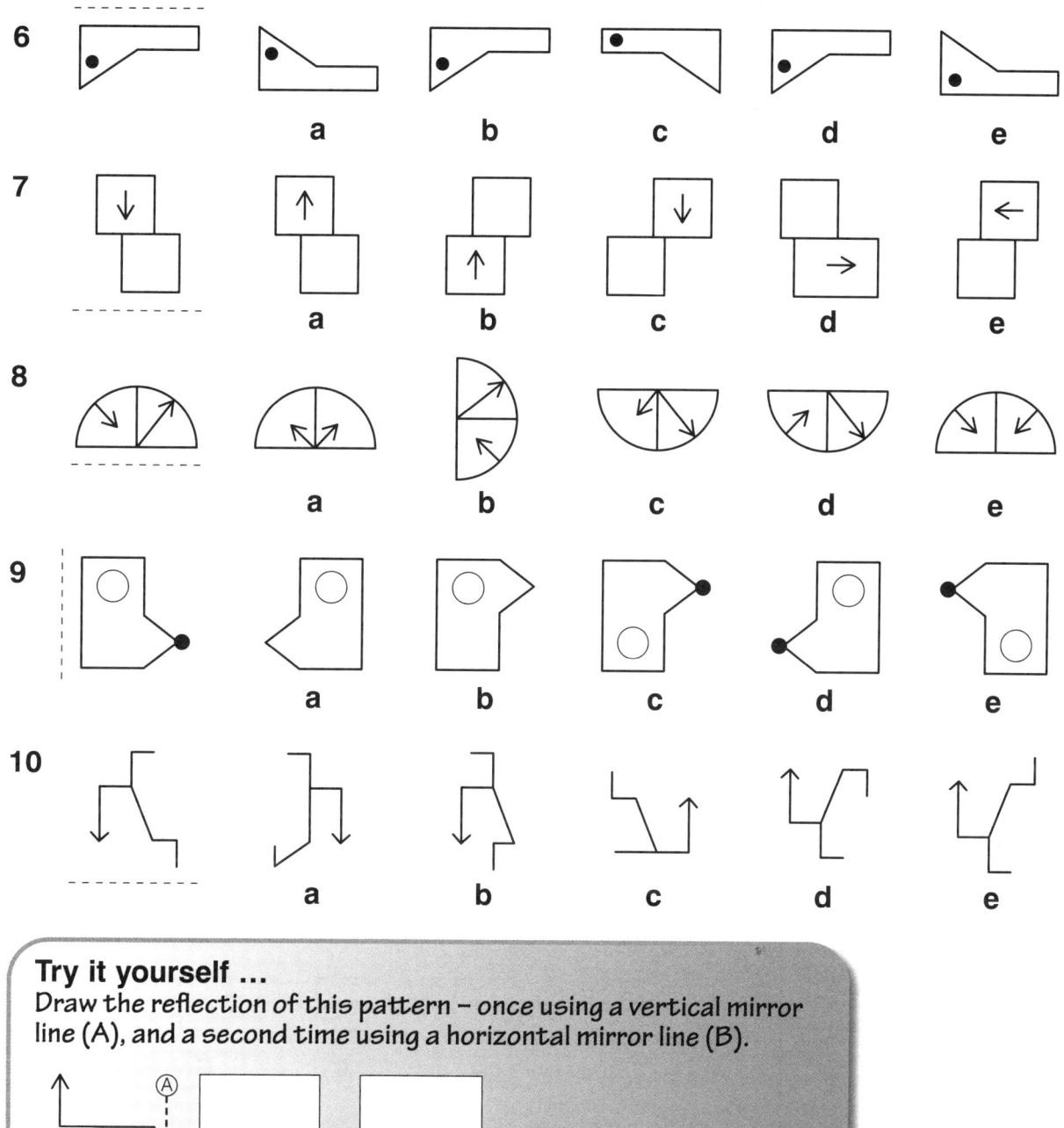

Focus test 5 — Grids

To find the picture that will complete the pattern, you have to look carefully at the grid. Does the whole grid form a pattern? Is it symmetrical? Is there a sequence going across the rows or down the columns? If more than one feature changes, you need to find the pattern for each feature – they may be different.

Which one completes the grid? Circle the letter.

Example

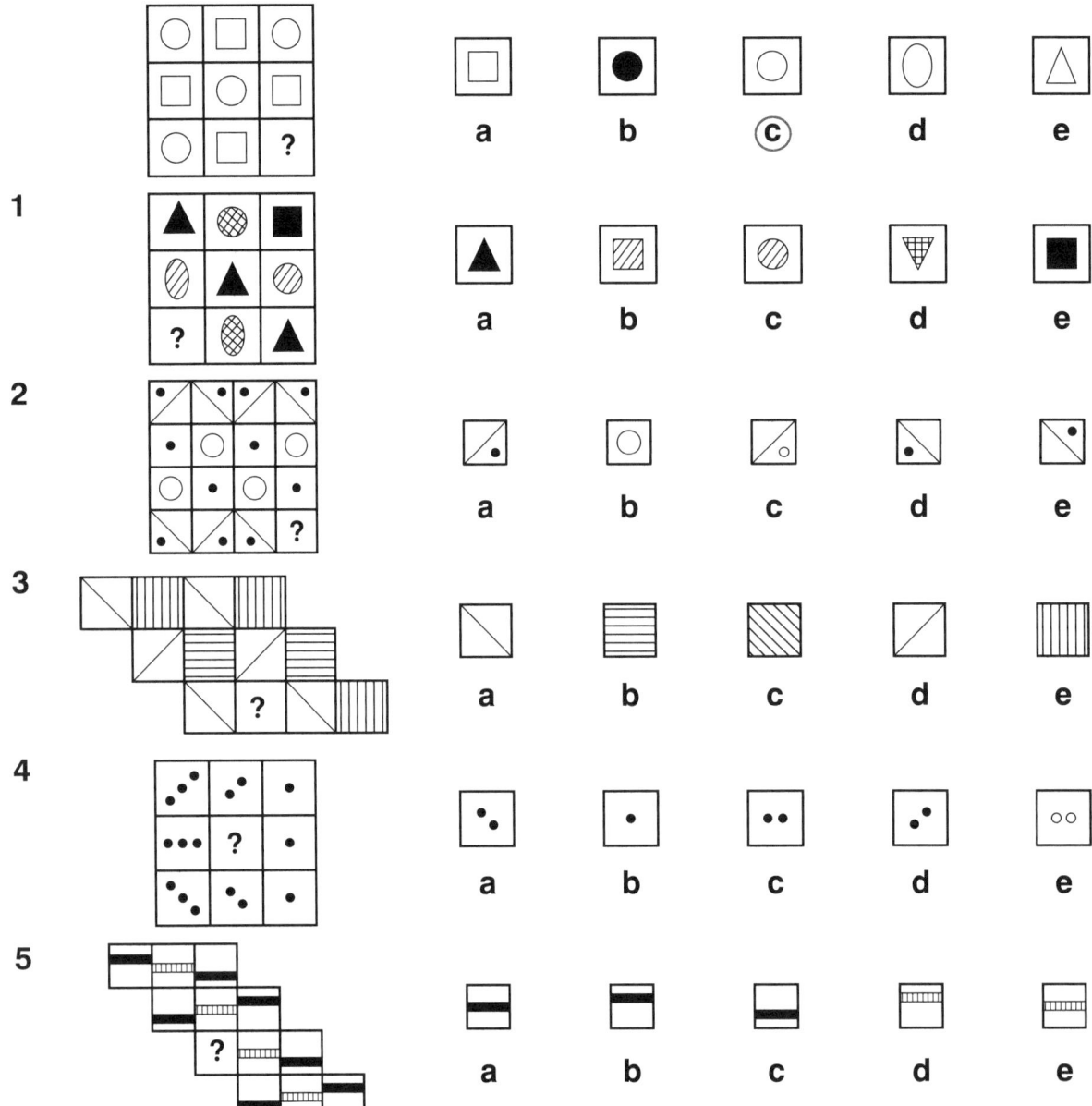

The grids are not always squares. Look carefully to see how the patterns in each shape relate to one another in order to find the missing part.

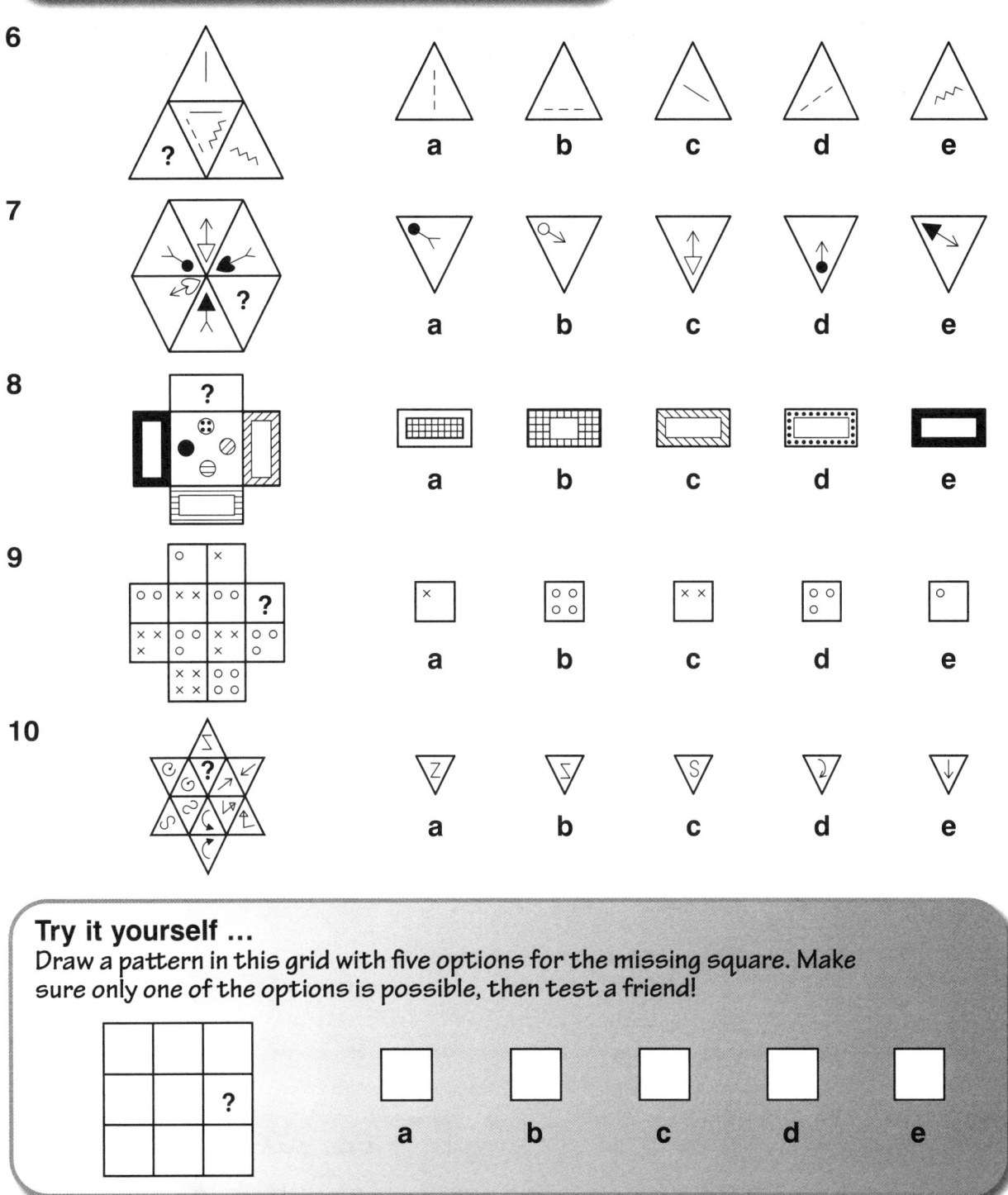

Try it yourself ...
Draw a pattern in this grid with five options for the missing square. Make sure only one of the options is possible, then test a friend!

Focus test 6 — Codes

When a set of shapes has codes, the first letter in the code always applies to the same feature in all of the shapes, such as number or shading. The second letter will apply to a different feature, such as size or position. Sometimes there are extra features in the shapes that do not link with the codes – identify them, then ignore them!

Which code matches the last shape? Circle the letter.

Example

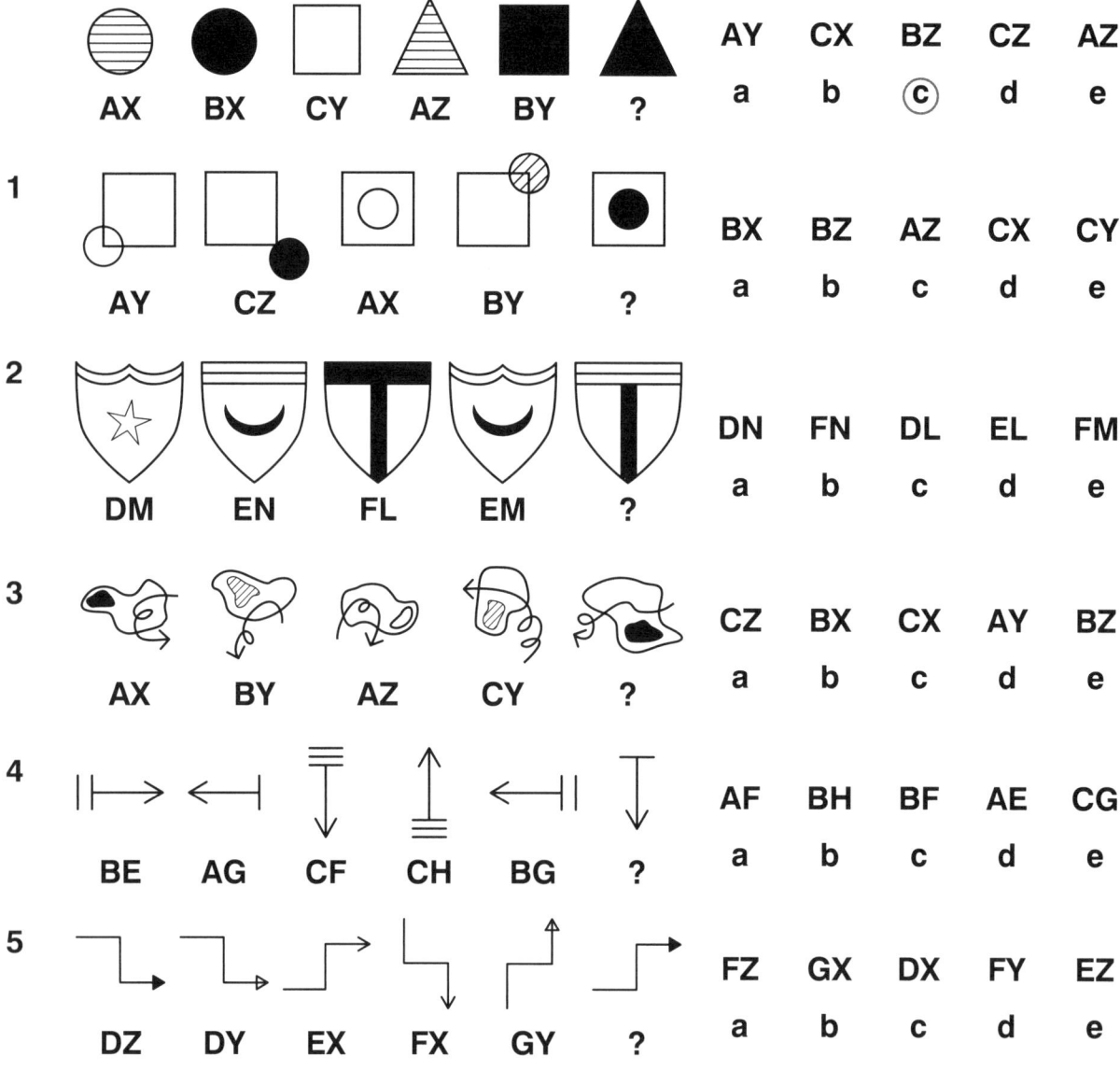

If there is only one shape for one of the letter codes, the feature to which it is linked must be worked out by deduction.

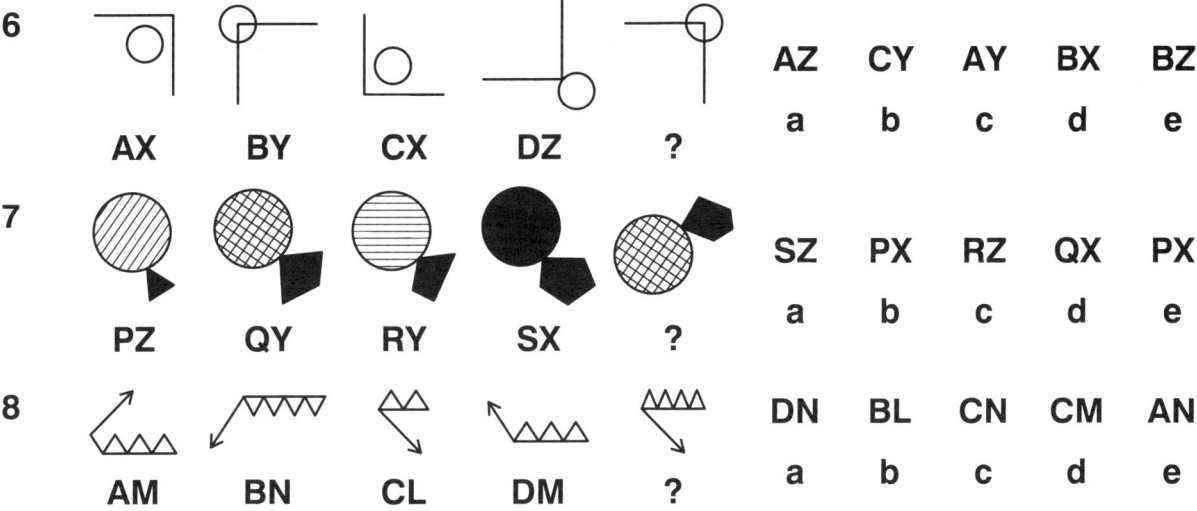

There can be three parts to some more challenging codes. To find the missing code, work through the same process, first looking at the shapes that have the same first letter to identify the first feature. Then repeat this for the second and third letters.

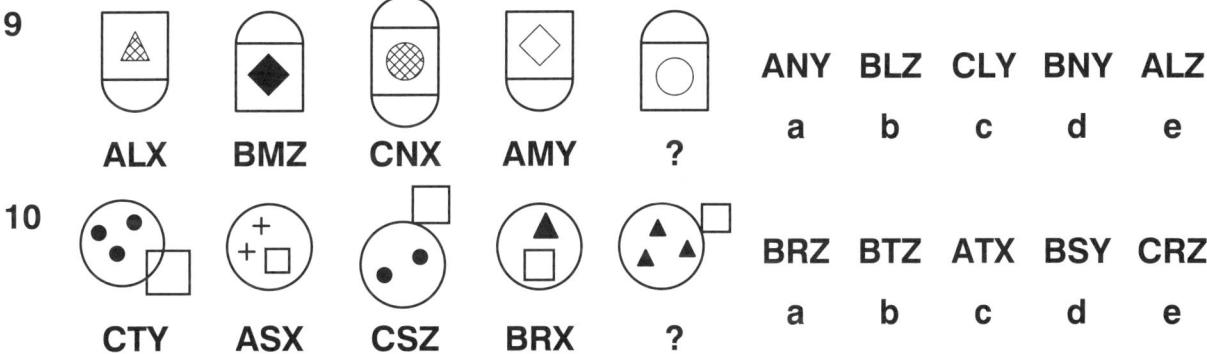

Try it yourself …
Draw a set of four shapes, give them codes and provide answer options. Remember that the first letter must link to the same characteristic and the second letter to another, different characteristic. For an extra challenge you could include a third letter. See if a friend can solve your question!

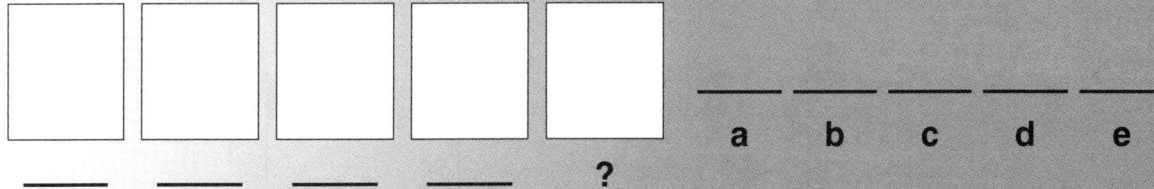

Now go to the Progress Chart … 15 … to record your score!   Total   10

Focus test 7 — Cubes

When the patterns used in cube questions have a direction, you have to work out which faces will end up next to each other in the cube <u>and</u> which way the pattern will be facing. Patterns such as ○, × or ■ do not have a direction but many do, for example ↑, ♥ and ☺. Identifying the edges that will end up next to each other can help you to work out the orientation of the pattern on each face.

Which of these nets will fold to give the cube on the left? Circle the letter.

Example

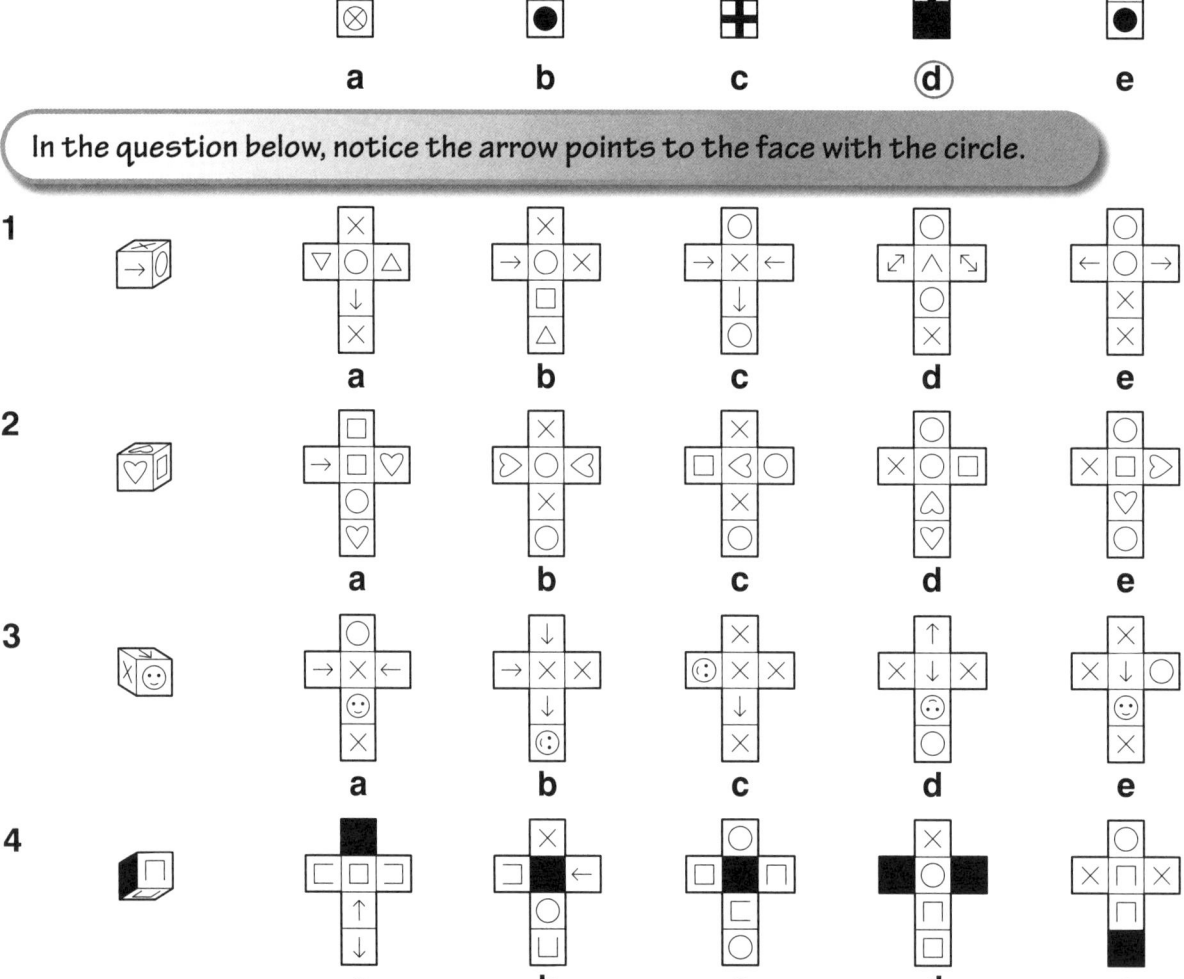

In the question below, notice the arrow points to the face with the circle.

Other nets can also fold up to give a cube – look carefully to see how they will fold, and notice which edges and faces end up next to each other.

5

a b c d e

6

a b c d e

7

a b c d e

8

a b c d e

9

a b c d e

10

a b c d e

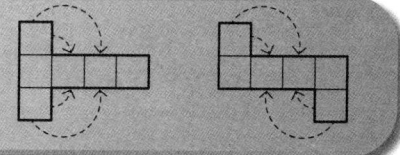

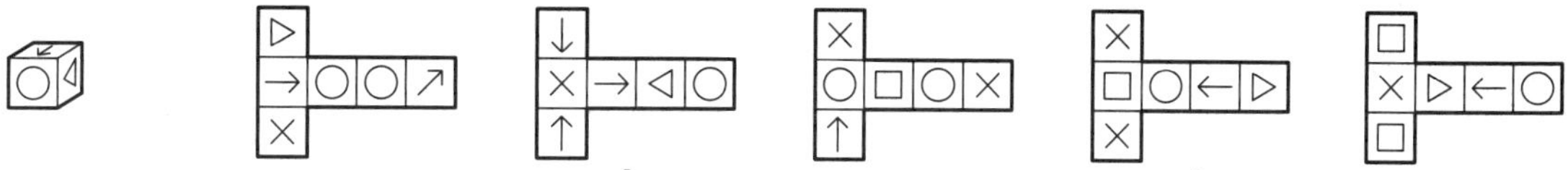

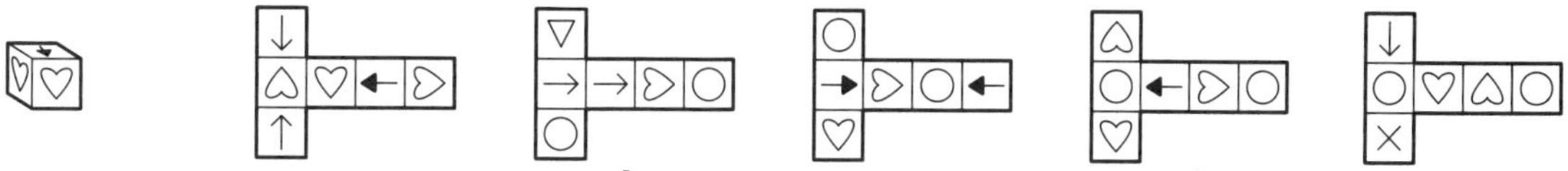

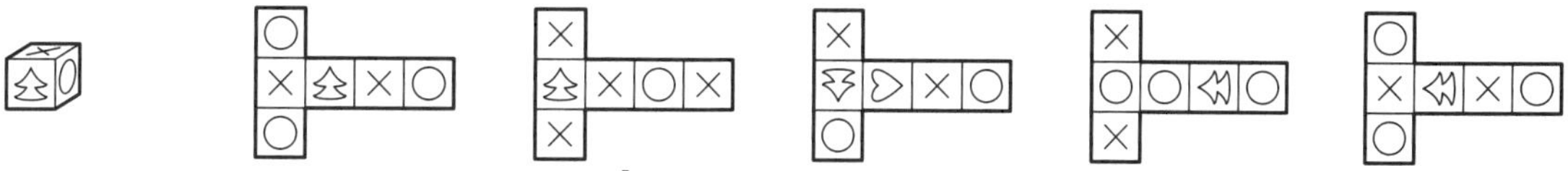

Try it yourself …

Draw a pattern on the three visible faces of this cube and then complete the five nets so that just <u>one</u> of them can be folded to make the cube. See if a friend can answer your question!

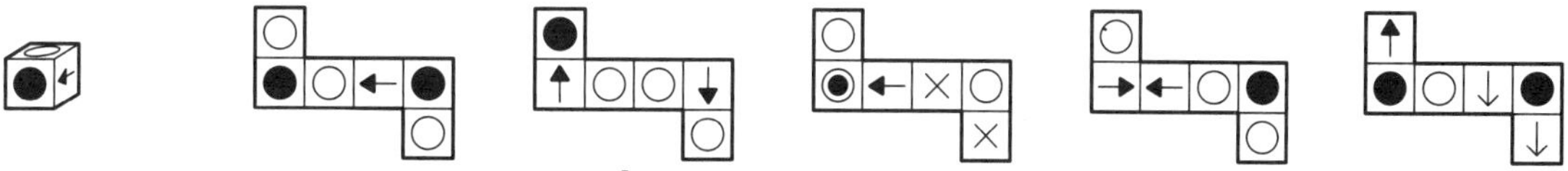

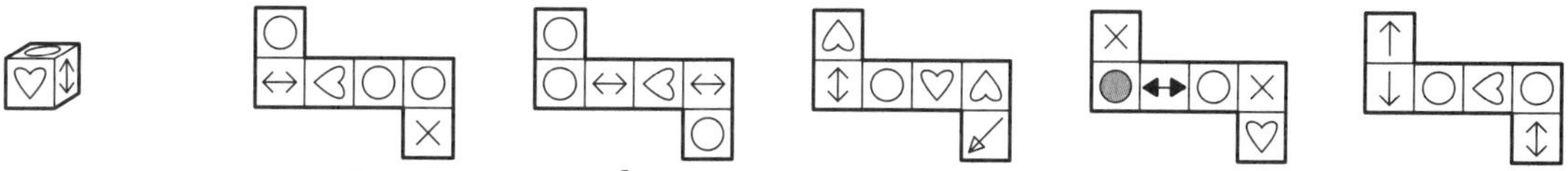

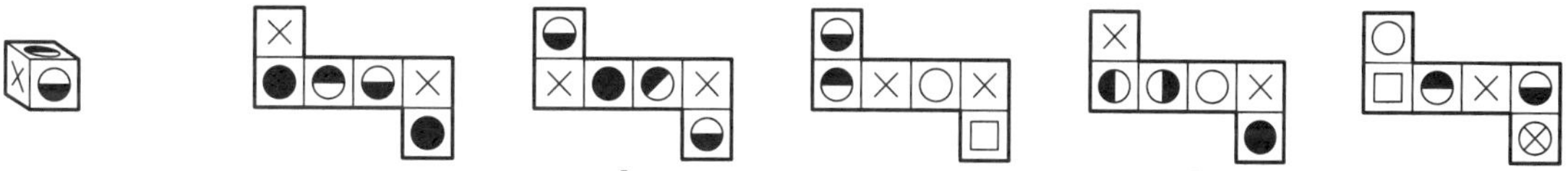

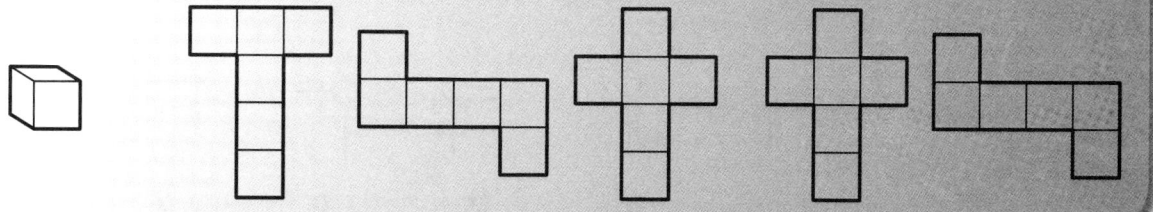

Focus test 8 — Combining shapes

When looking through the answer options for these questions, remember that the two separate shapes can be rotated either way in the new combined shape, but cannot be flipped over. If a shape is rotated, this may affect the angle of any shading lines.

Which pattern is made by combining the two shapes on the left? Circle the letter.

Example

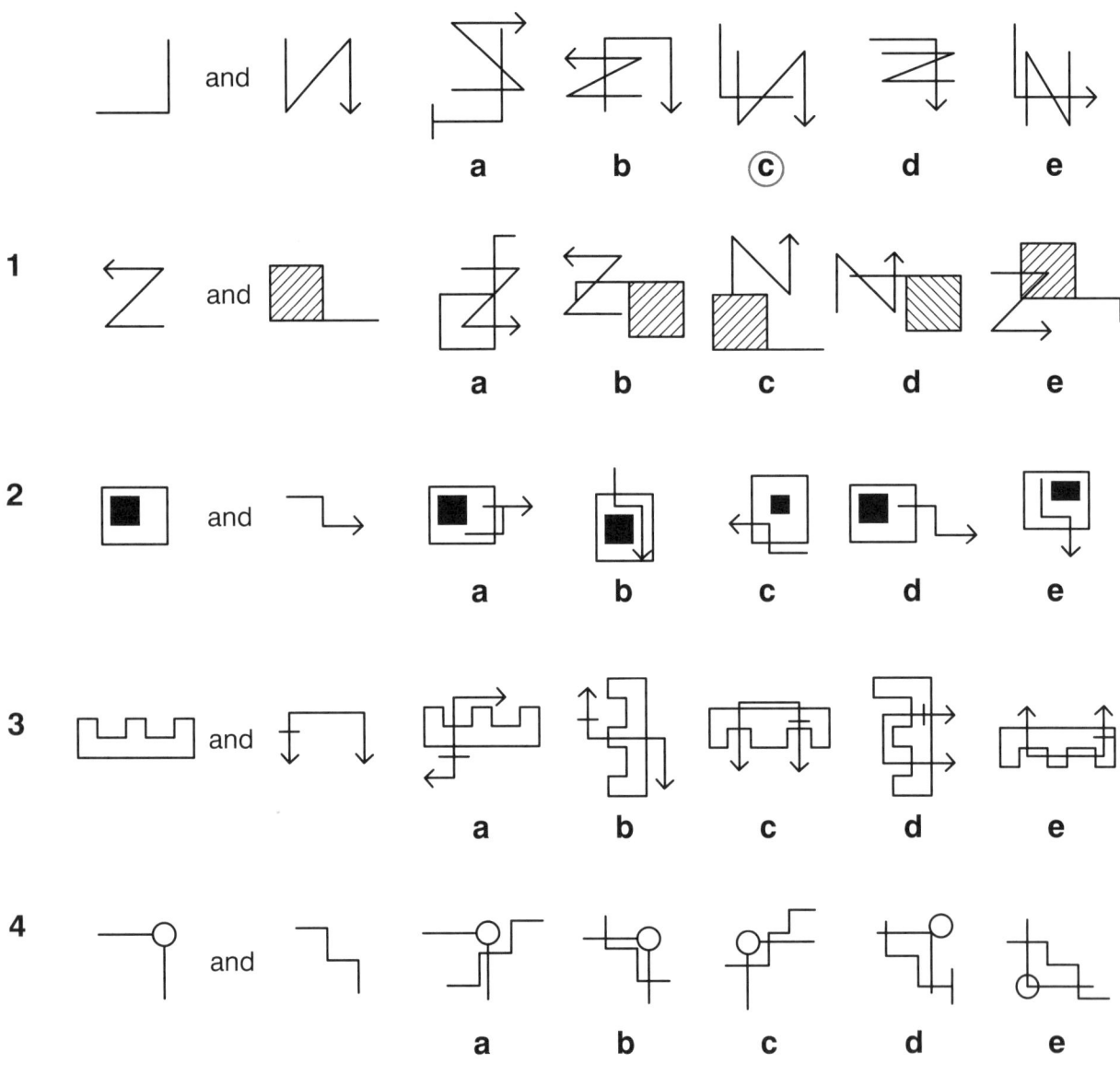

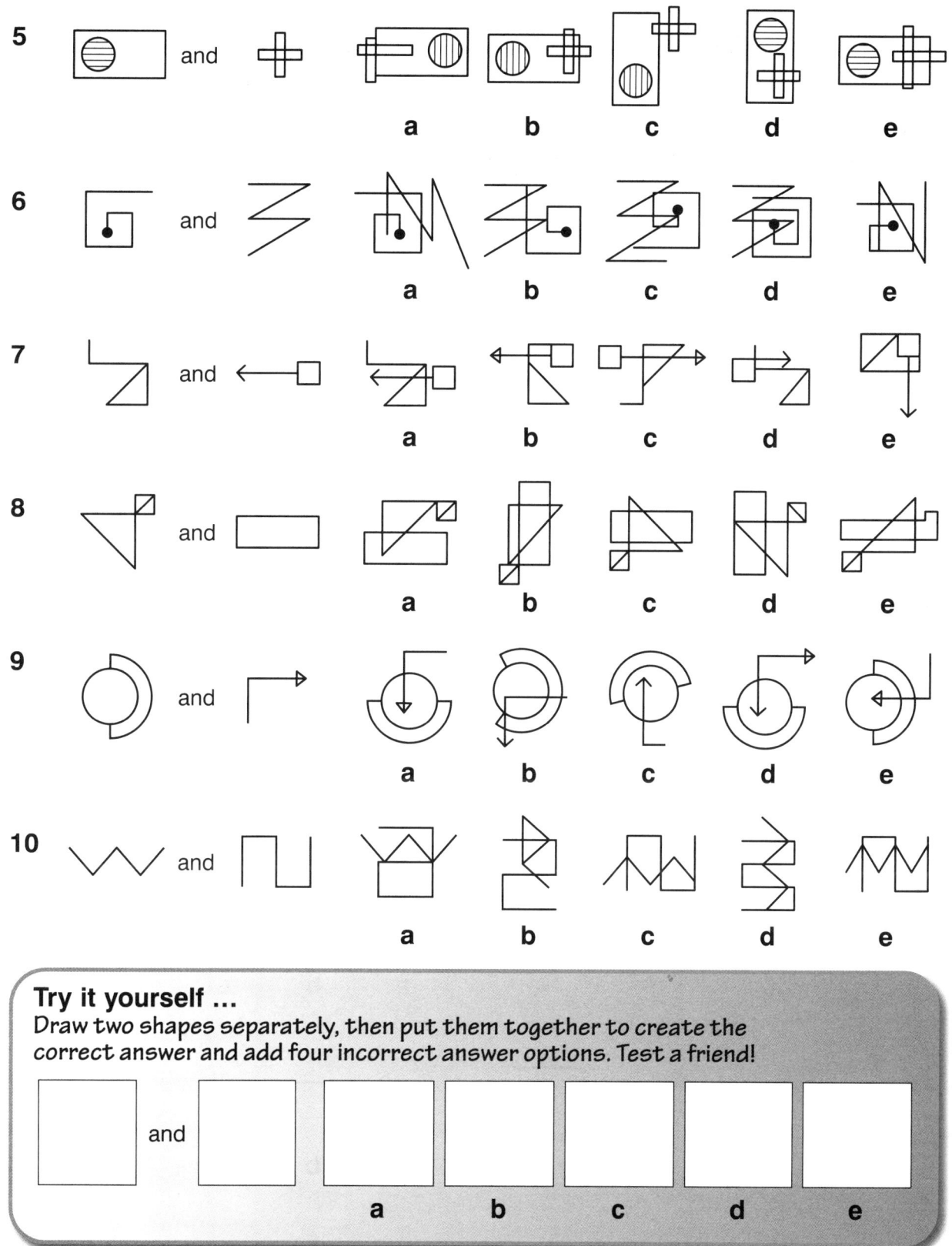

Focus test 9 — Shape

This test looks at how SHAPE can be a key characteristic in different question types. It may be important to identify the shape of a whole pattern, or it may be important to notice the shape of different elements or parts within a pattern. Shape may be a characteristic on its own, or it may be combined with another characteristic to form a significant feature in a question, so remember to look very carefully and notice every detail.

Which one belongs to the group on the left? Circle the letter.

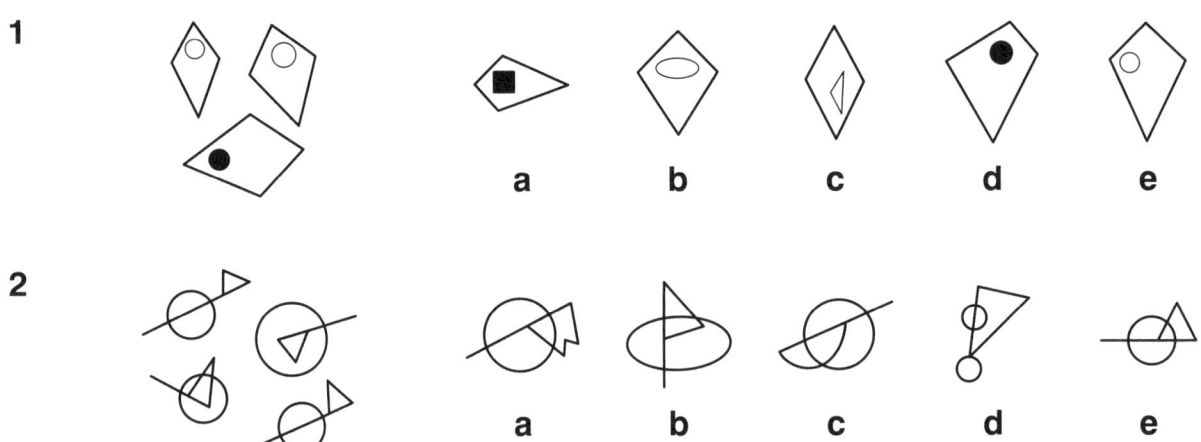

Which one completes the second pair in the same way as the first pair? Circle the letter.

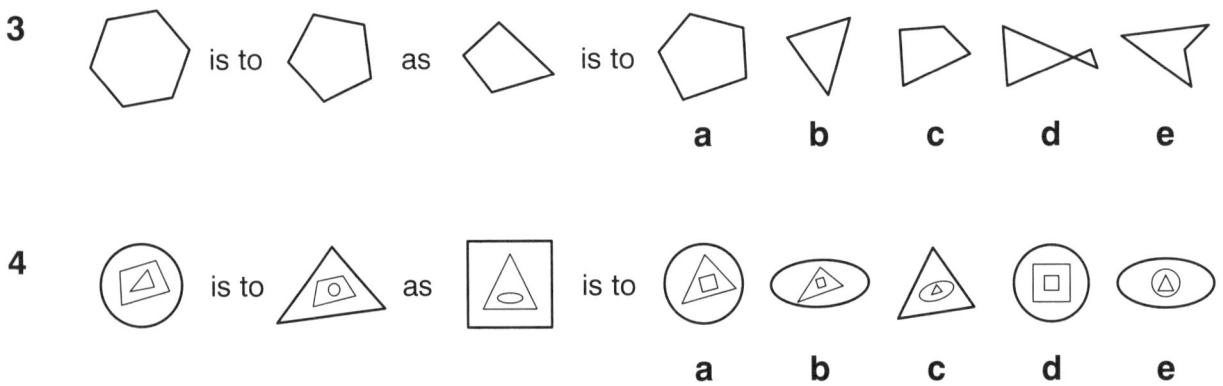

20

Which one completes the sequence? Circle the letter.

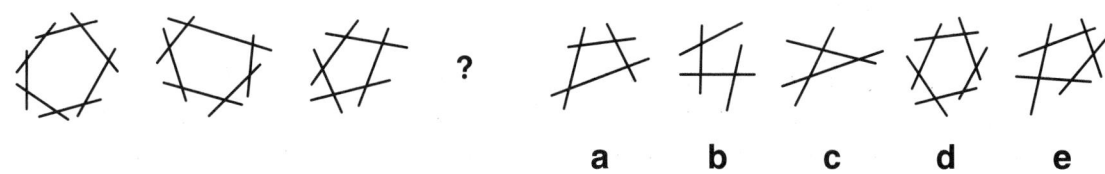

Which one is a reflection of the pattern on the left? Circle the letter.

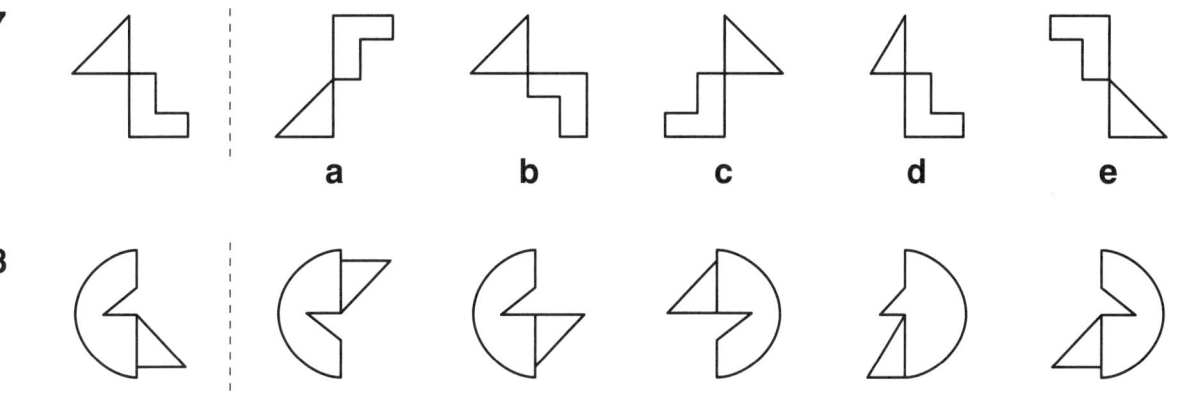

Which code matches the last shape? Circle the letter.

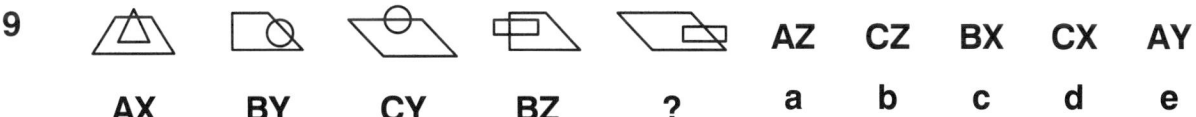

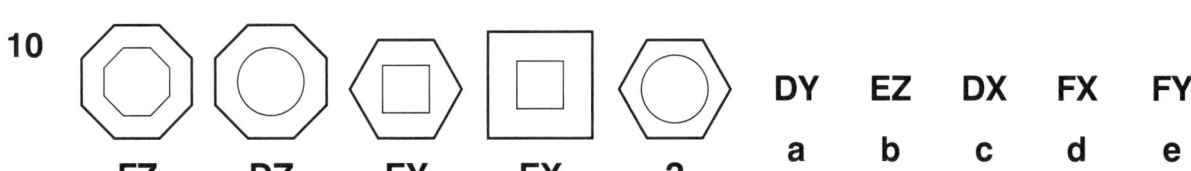

Focus test 10 — Position

In these questions, the important part to notice in each pattern is the POSITION of each element. The linking position between two or more parts will be the clue to finding the correct answer option.

Which one belongs to the group on the left? Circle the letter.

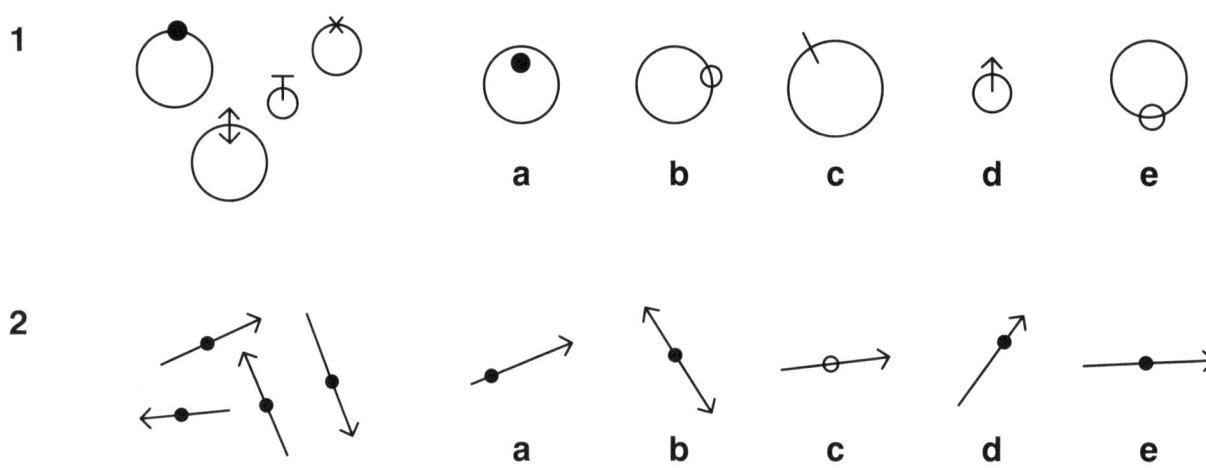

Which one completes the second pair in the same way as the first pair? Circle the letter.

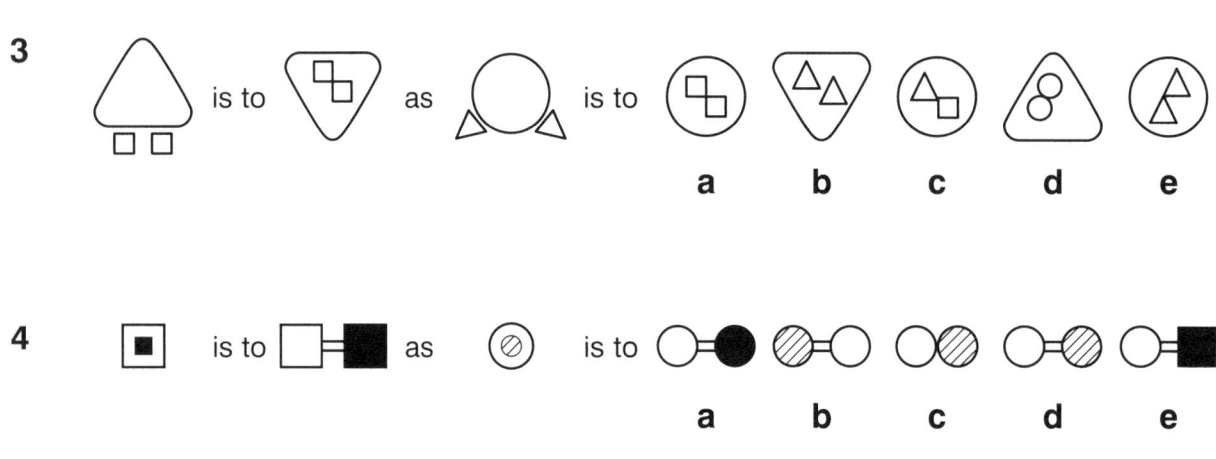

Which one completes the sequence? Circle the letter.

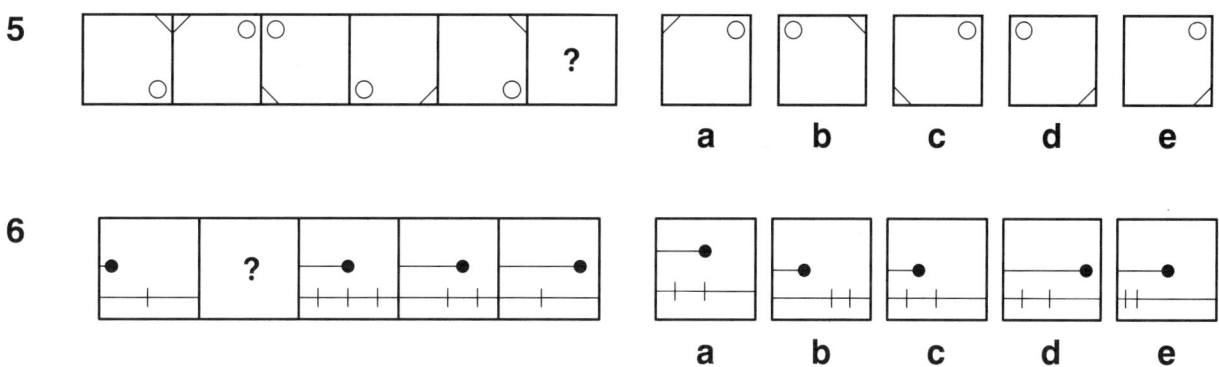

Which one completes the grid? Circle the letter.

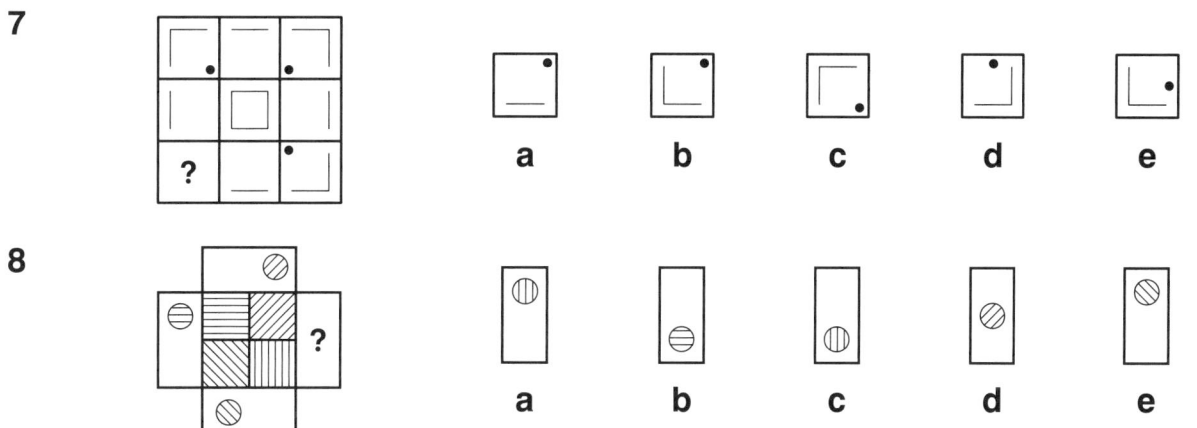

Which code matches the last shape? Circle the letter.

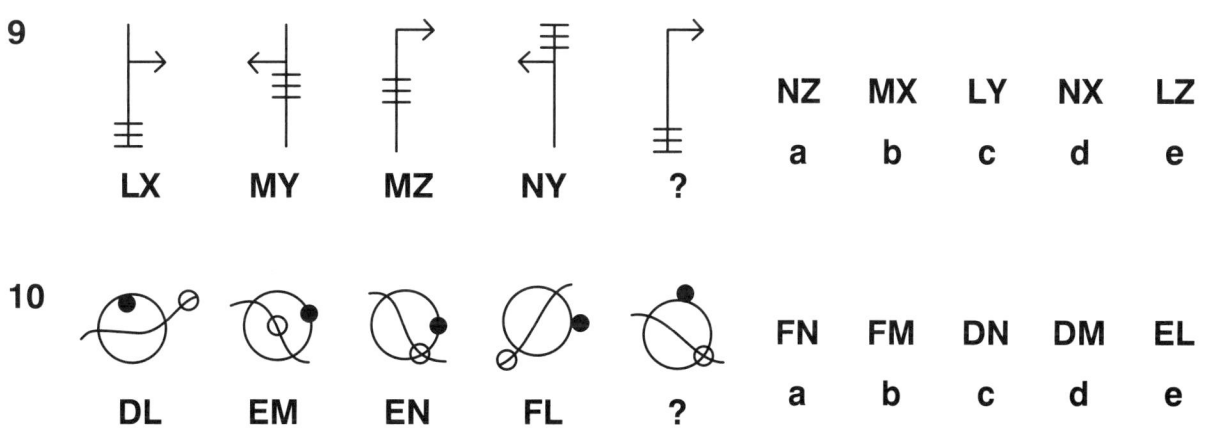

Now go to the Progress Chart ... 23 *... to record your score!* Total 10

Focus test 11 — Angle

In this test, the patterns focus on the actual ANGLE made in each picture. It is helpful to be able to recognise the following angle types easily and accurately.

acute   right angle (corner)   obtuse

Half a right angle (45°) is a commonly used acute angle.

Thinking of a compass can help you to recognise 45° and 90° angles.

A clock face gives angles of 30° in the centre, so imagining lines as the hands of a clock can help you identify angles.

Which one belongs to the group on the left? Circle the letter.

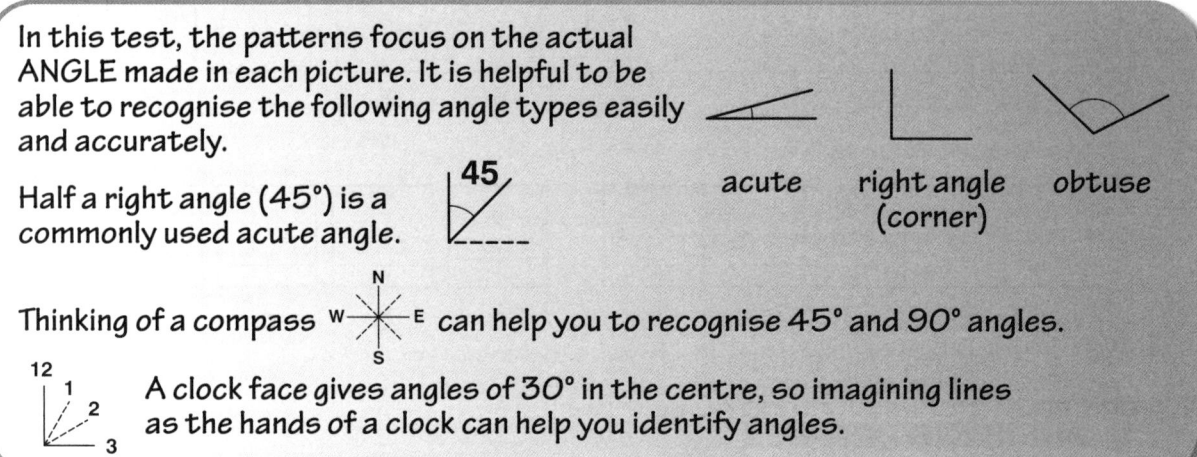

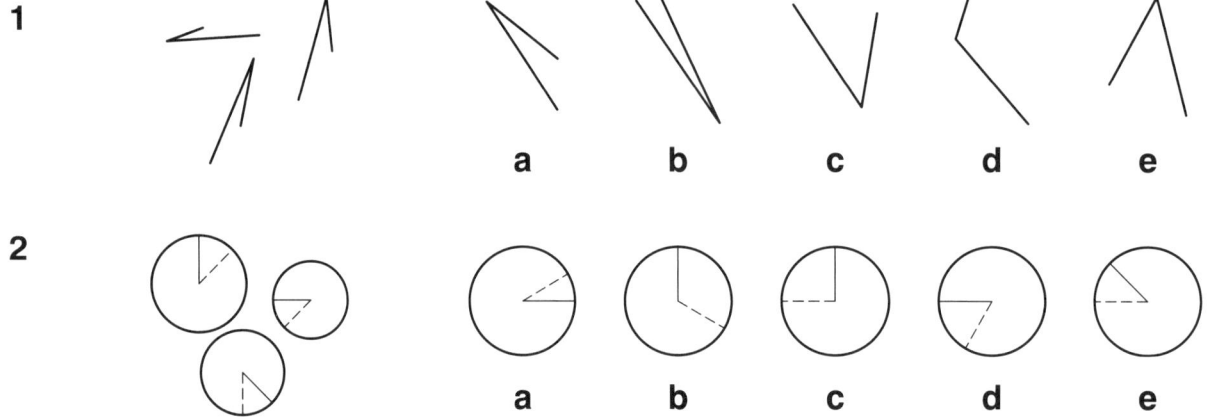

Which one completes the second pair in the same way as the first pair? Circle the letter.

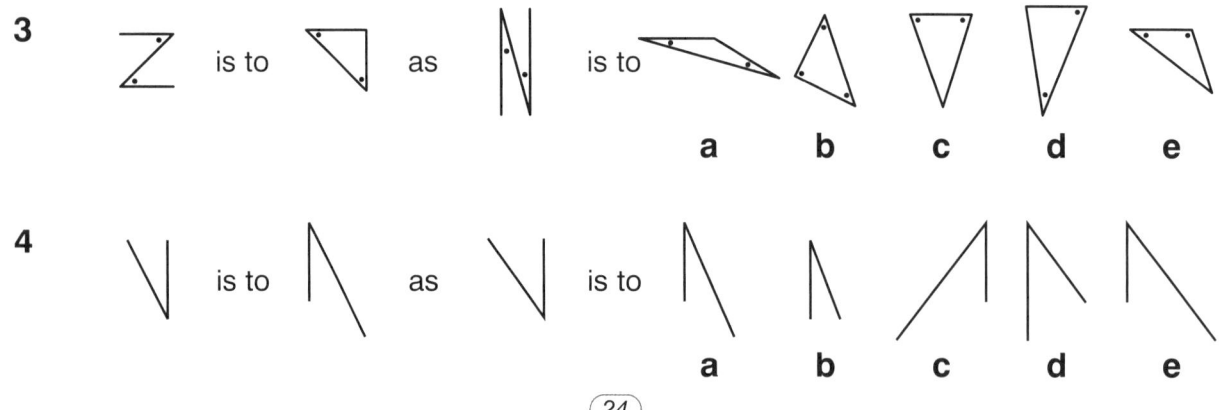

Which one completes the sequence? Circle the letter.

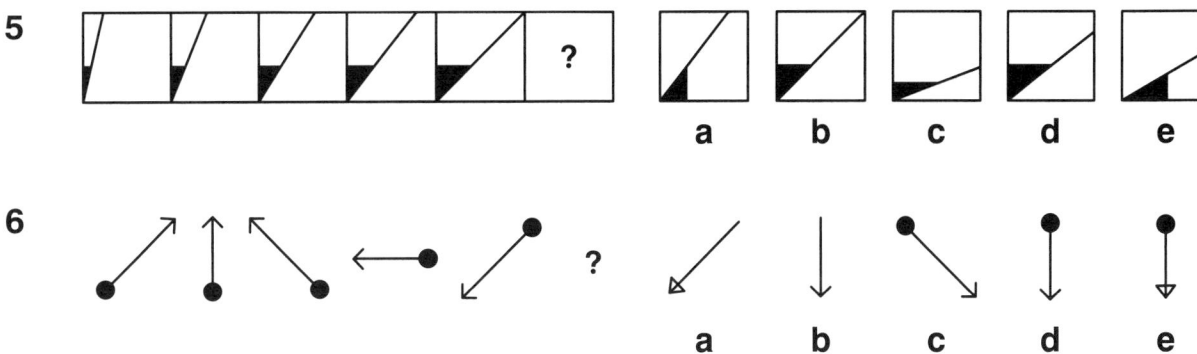

Which one is a reflection of the pattern on the left? Circle the letter.

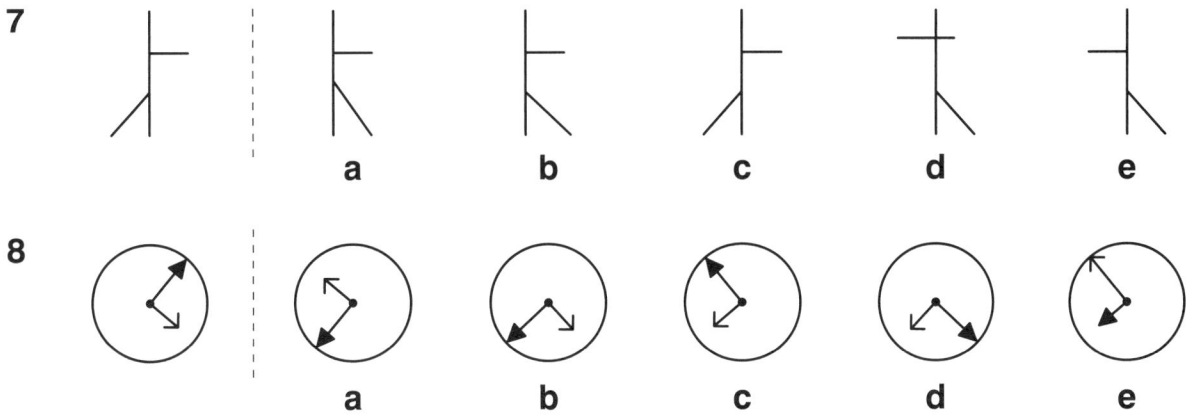

Which code matches the last shape? Circle the letter.

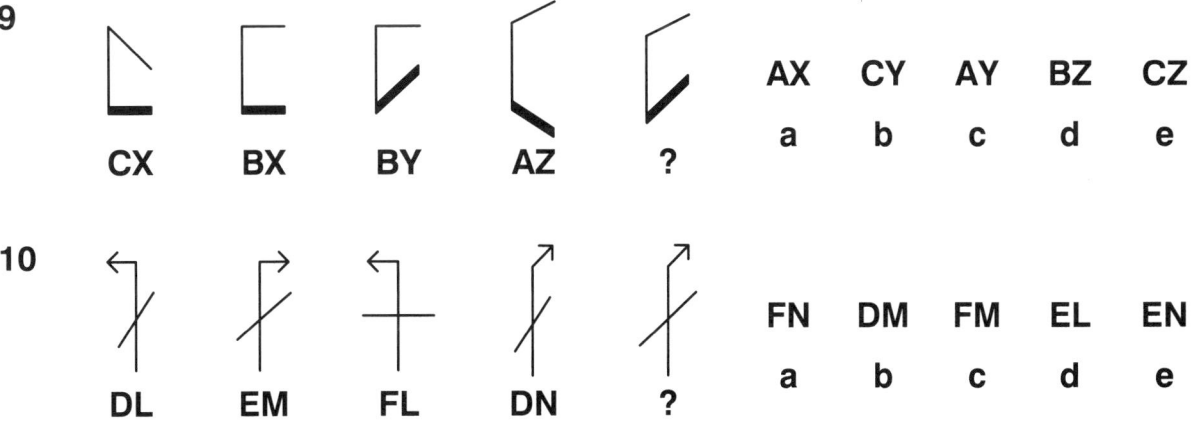

Focus test 12 — Number

Questions will often involve NUMBER – this may be the total number of lines, objects or angles. It may be a pattern relating to number – increasing, alternating, doubling or decreasing.

Which one belongs to the group on the left? Circle the letter.

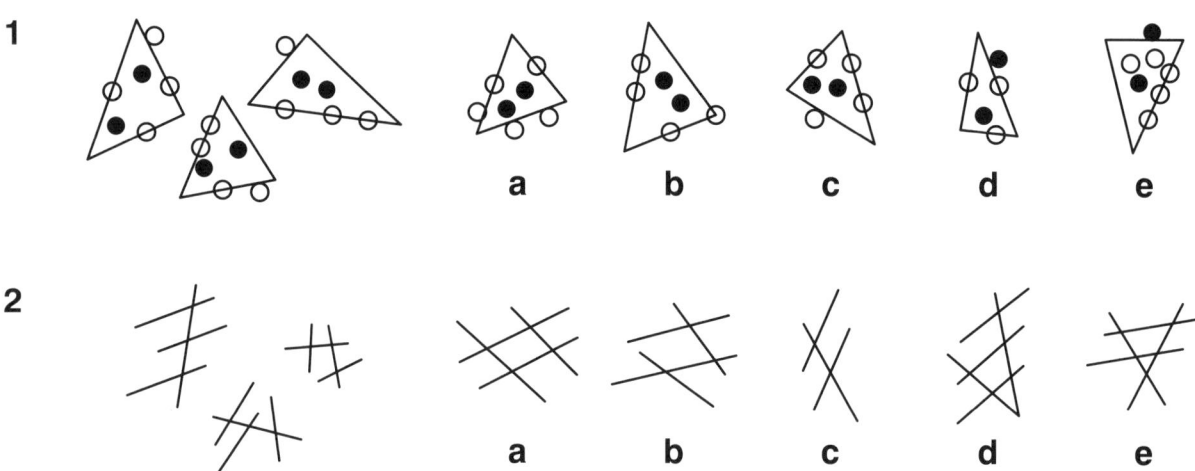

Which one completes the second pair in the same way as the first pair? Circle the letter.

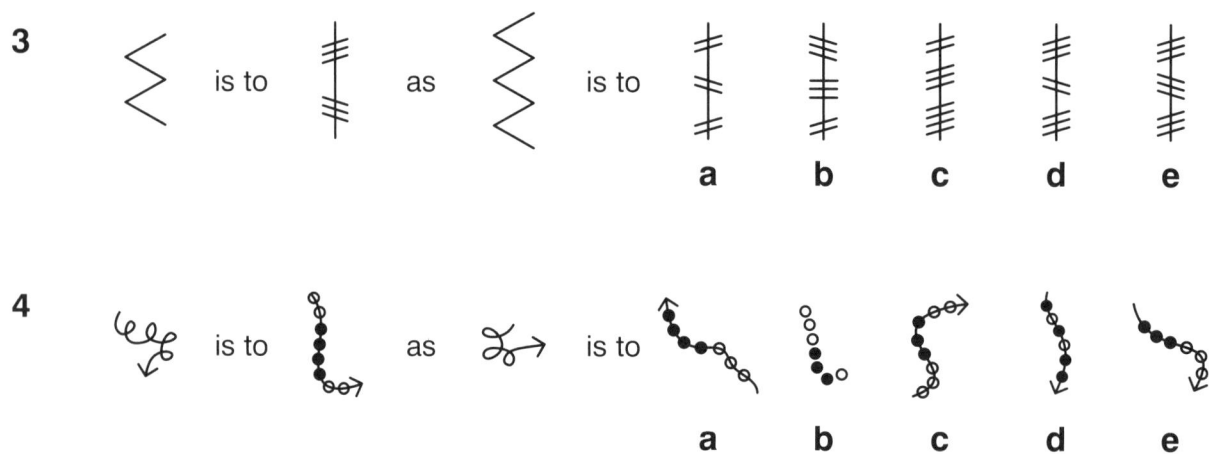

Focus test 1: Similarities (pages 4–5)

1. **d** All of the shapes on the left have the same sized circle with a straight 'stem' between.
2. **b** All of the shapes on the left are right-angled triangles with two spots inside them.
3. **e** All of the shapes on the left have diagonal line shading and one black circle outside the shape touching the curved line.
4. **c** All of the shapes on the left have three short lines in a zig-zag with a black circle at one end.
5. **e** All of the shapes on the left are triangles with either a small black triangle or a small white circle inside.
6. **d** All of the shapes on the left are quadrilaterals with cross-hatch shading and a black circle, which may be on the outside touching a corner, or inside the quadrilateral.
7. **d** All of the shapes on the left are circles with a single headed arrow going across them, both starting and ending outside the circle.
8. **e** All of the patterns on the left are made up of one curved line with one straight line crossing it once.
9. **d** All of the shapes on the left are crescents.
10. **b** All of the patterns on the left are made up of five touching shapes with one of the five shaded black.

Focus test 2: Analogies (pages 6–7)

1. **e** The second shape is the first shape rotated through a half turn (180°) and with the solid lines changed to dashed lines.
2. **c** The shape on the right fits into the shape on the left to form a rectangle.
3. **d** In the second pattern, the L-shape becomes a complete square and the small black shape becomes white and moves to the position diagonally opposite and within the square.
4. **c** The second pattern is the inner shape of the first pattern with the shading style of the outer shape of the first pattern.
5. **d** The second pattern is the shape of the first pattern shaded black, with four of the original shape (which stays white) around the outside.
6. **b** The second pattern is the image of the first shape reflected in a vertical mirror line.
7. **e** The second pattern is the shape of the first pattern rotated through a half turn (180°).
8. **b** In the second pattern the square becomes a circle, and the segment opposite the black section of the first pattern is shaded with cross-hatch shading while the black segment becomes white.
9. **a** The second pattern is the two white shapes in the first pattern within each other, and the small black shape in the centre.
10. **b** The second pattern is the "negative" of the first pattern: all of the white sections become black, and the black sections become white.

Focus test 3: Sequences (pages 8–9)

1. **c** The upside down U-shapes alternate with V-shapes; the V-shapes are alternately pointing up or down. Also, the circle inside the U-shapes alternates between black and white but this is not part of the solution here.
2. **e** The number of short lines across the arrows has a repeating pattern of 3–2–1–; the arrows rotate through a quarter turn (90°) anticlockwise each time; and the arrowhead follows the pattern open–unshaded–open–shaded–.
3. **d** The rows of black circles alternate orientation by a quarter turn (90°); the black circle rows alternate with the dotted circle rows; and the dotted circle rows alternate orientation by a quarter turn (90°).
4. **a** The spots increase by one each time; the short line extending from the square rotates by a quarter turn (90°) at each corner before moving to the next corner in an anticlockwise direction.
5. **c** The zig-zag pattern alternates with the pattern of circles; the overall pattern is decreasing by one each time so the number of circles is one less than the lines in the zig-zag to its left.
6. **e** Circles and squares alternate along each row of five linked shapes; the top shape is always shaded black and one shape has diagonal shading top right–bottom left, and along the sequence alternate patterns commence with a black circle or a black square.
7. **a** The small inner shapes follow a repeating pattern of circle–square–triangle, shaded alternately black or white. The position of the small shape moves round the inner corners of the large square in an anticlockwise direction, one corner each time.
8. **b** The arrows on the circles move a quarter turn (90°) clockwise around the outer edge of the circles, and the black spots move round the outside of the squares in the same way. The circles and squares alternate.
9. **d** The number of circles crossing the line of the irregular shapes increases by one each time. The outside and inside shapes are not part of the answer here.
10. **b** The position of the circle on the base line follows the repeating sequence left–middle–right, and the triangle shading follows the sequence –diagonal lines bottom left to top right–diagonal cross-hatched lines–diagonal lines top left to bottom right.

Focus test 4: Reflections (pages 10–11)

1 e
2 c
3 b
4 d
5 e
6 a
7 b
8 d

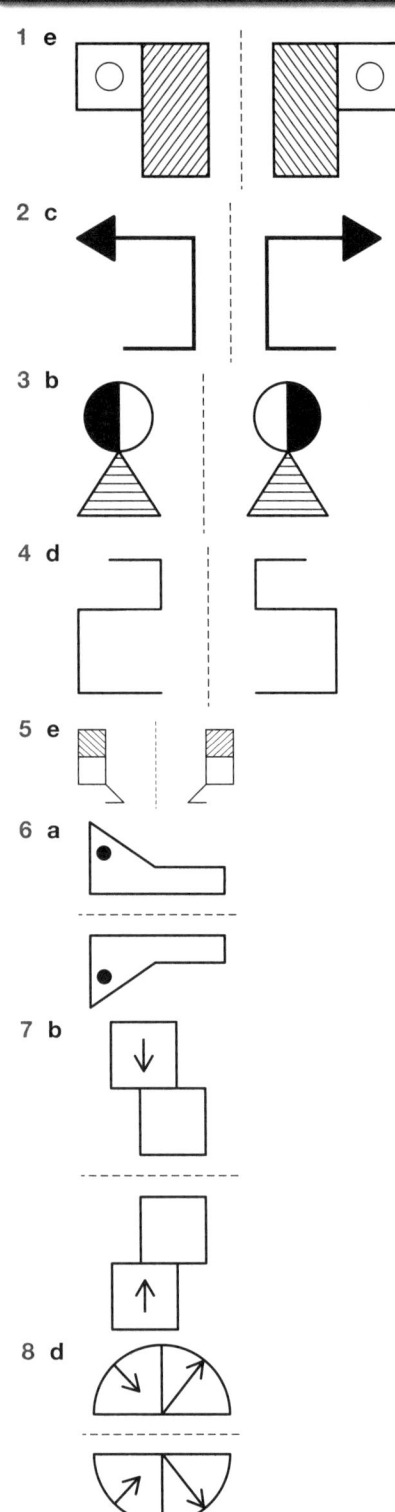

9 d
10 e

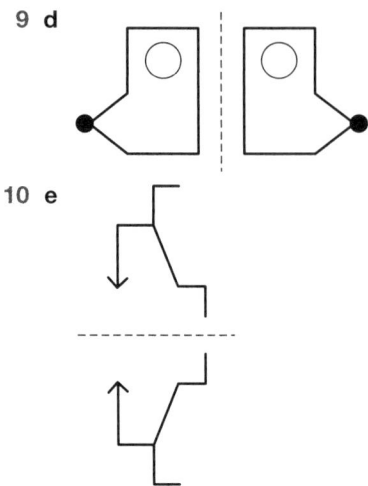

Focus test 5: Grids (pages 12–13)

1 **e** From left to right along each row and then down onto the next row, the pattern is triangle–circle–square–oval, with shading pattern of –black–cross hatch–black–diagonal line–.
2 **a** The bottom row of the grid is a reflection of the top row.
3 **e** The bottom row of the grid is a repeat of the top row; each row is offset one place.
4 **c** The spots along each row follow the orientation of the three spots in the first square, and they decrease in number by one each time across the row.
5 **b** The pattern in the third row is the same as the pattern in the first row but moved along two squares to the right. The shaded lines follow the pattern above–on–below the centre line on the first and third rows and below–on–above in the second and fourth rows.
6 **d** Each of the three lines in the inner triangle are copied into the triangle adjoining them, perpendicular to the shared side.
7 **b** Opposite patterns in the hexagon are nearly the same, but one of each pair has black shading while the other is white, and one of each pair has an arrowhead while the other has a V-shape.
8 **d** The shading around the edge of each rectangle is the same as the shading of the adjacent inner circle.
9 **c** The number of crosses or circles is the same along each row, with crosses and circles alternating.
10 **a** The pattern in each of the outer triangles is a reflection of the pattern inside the adjacent triangle.

Focus test 6: Codes (pages 14–15)

1–10 Even though the explanations below give the letters in order, you may find it easier to identify features linking the second letter and then move on to the first letter.

1. **d** The first letter represents the shading of the circle (A is white, B is lines, C is black); the second letter represents the position of the circle in relation to the square (X in the middle, Y over a corner, Z outside).

2. **b** The first letter represents the pattern in the middle of the shield shape (D is a star, E a crescent, F a vertical black line); the second letter represents the line style at the top of the shield (L is black, M is a curved double line, N is a straight triple line).

3. **b** The first letter represents the number and position of the loops on the curved line (A is one inside the shape, B is one outside the shape, C is two outside the shape); the second letter represents the shading of the inner small shape (X is black, Y is lines, Z is white).

4. **a** The first letter represents the number of short lines across the end of the arrow (A is 1, B is 2, C is 3); the second letter represents the direction of the arrow (E points to the right, F points down, G points to the left, H points up).

5. **e** The first letter represents the orientation of the 'stepped' line (D starts top left and ends pointing right, E starts bottom left and ends pointing right, F starts top left and ends pointing down, G starts bottom left and ends pointing up); the second letter represents the arrowhead (X is open, Y an unshaded triangle, Z a black triangle).

6. **c** The first letter represents the orientation of the L-shaped line (A has corner at top right, B has corner at top left, C has corner at bottom left, D has corner at bottom right); the second letter represents the position of the circle (X within the L-shape, Y over the corner, Z outside the corner).

7. **d** The first letter represents the shading style of the circle (P is diagonal lines, Q is cross-hatched, R is horizontal lines, S is black); the second letter represents the number of sides on the outer black shape (X is 5, Y is 4, Z is 3).

8. **c** The first letter represents the direction of the arrow (A pointing top right, B pointing bottom left, C pointing bottom right, D pointing top left); the second letter represents the number of triangles on the horizontal line (L is 2, M is 3, N is 4).

9. **d** The first letter represents the number and position of the white semi-circles (A one below the square, B one above the square, C has one above and one below); the second letter represents the shape inside the rectangle (L a triangle, M a rhombus, N a circle); the third letter represents the shading style of the inner shape (X is cross-hatched, Y is white, Z is black).

10. **b** The first letter represents the shape in addition to the circle and square (A is a cross, B a triangle, C a circle); the second letter represents the number of these shapes (R is 1, S is 2, T is 3); the third letter represents the position of the square (X inside the circle, Y over the circle edge, Z outside the circle).

Focus test 7: Cubes (pages 16–17)

1. **b** The arrow has to point to a face with a circle (**b** or **c**) and have a cross on the face adjacent to it.

2. **d** The two hearts have their top curved edges along the same edge of the cube.

3. **e** Only one net has an arrow pointing to the top of the 'smiley face'.

4. **c** The two faces with the square U-shape have the open side of the U opposite each other, along the same edge of the cube.

5. **a** The top of the triangle and the arrow must both point to a face with a circle.

6. **c** The face with the black arrow points to the top of the face with the heart. The two hearts are adjacent and the same way up.

7. **e** The face with the 'tree' shape points to a face with an X (**b** or **e**) and is next to a face with a circle (**c** or **e**).

8. **b** The solid-headed arrow points to the face with the black circle.

9. **e** The top of the heart is along the edge of a face with a white circle (**a** or **e**) and the heart face is next to the double arrow (**c** or **e**).

10. **d** The two faces with the half-shaded circles have the white half of each circle along the shared edge between them.

Focus test 8: Combining shapes (pages 18–19)

1 c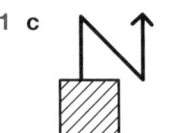

2 d

3 e

4 b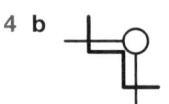

5 c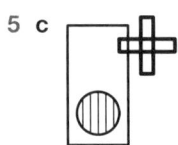

6 b

7 a

8 c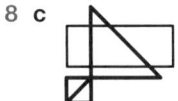

9 e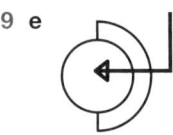

10 c

Focus test 9: Shape (pages 20–21)

1 **e** All of the shapes on the left are kites with circles inside them. A kite has two pairs of equal sides.

2 **e** All of the shapes on the left are made up of triangular 'flags' and circles.

3 **b** The second shape in each pair has one side less than the first shape.

4 **b** The outside shape and the centre shape in the first pattern swap places (and size) to give the second pattern.

5 **a** The number of lines decreases by one each time which also reduces the number of sides of the enclosed shape.

6 **d** The shapes at the right end of the line follow the repeating sequence –triangle with right angle in middle of line–small square–triangle with right angle at the end of the line–. The sixth shape will be the same as the third.

7 c

8 e

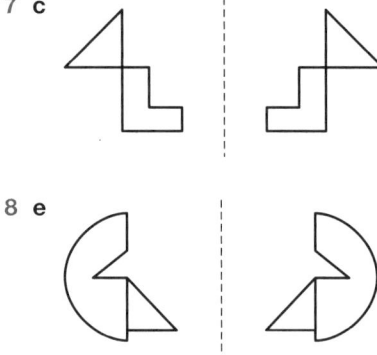

9–10 Even though the explanations below give the letters in order, you may find it easier to identify features linking the second letter and then move on to the first letter.

9 **b** The first letter represents the type of larger quadrilateral (A is a trapezium, B a right-angled trapezium, C a parallelogram); the second letter represents the overlapping shape (X a triangle, Y a circle, Z a rectangle).

10 **a** The first letter represents the inner shape (D a circle, E a square, F an octagon); the second letter represents the outer shape (X a square, Y a hexagon, Z an octagon).

Focus test 10: Position (pages 22–23)

1 **d** All of the circles on the left have a shape or line pattern crossing the circle at the top.

2 **e** All of the arrows on the left have a black spot half way along the line and only one arrow head.

3 **e** The small shapes below the large shape in the first pattern move inside the large shape and are touching in the second pattern.

4 **d** The inner shape in the first pattern increases to match the size of the outer shape; it sits on the right and is linked to the left-hand shape by a small white rectangle to give the second pattern.

5 **a** The triangle and the circle move anticlockwise around the inner corners of the square. The sixth box will be the same as the second.
6 **c** The line from the edge of the square to the black circle increases in length across the sequence; the number of equidistant short vertical lines crossing the line near the bottom of the square follows the pattern –1–2–3–2–1– .
7 **b** The corner squares of the grid have the right angle of the L-shape in the outer corner with the black spot diagonally opposite. The grid has symmetry across its diagonals.
8 **c** The circle in the outer rectangles moves clockwise around the grid keeping the same position within the rectangle and having the same shading as the adjacent inner square.
9–10 Even though the following explanations give the letters in order, you may find it easier to identify features linking the second letter and then move on to the first letter.
9 **e** The first letter represents the position of the three short lines across the vertical line (L is bottom, M is middle, N is top); the second letter represents the position and direction of the arrow (X pointing right below the top, Y pointing left below the top, Z pointing right at the top).
10 **a** The first letter represents the position of the small black circle in relation to the large circle (D inside, E on the line, F outside); the second letter represents the position of the small white circle in relation to the large circle (L is outside, M is inside, N is on the line).

Focus test 11: Angle (pages 24–25)

1 **a** All of the shapes on the left have two lines forming an acute angle with one line much longer than the other.
2 **e** All of the circles on the left have a sector with 45° at the centre and one plain line and one dotted line.
3 **a** The equal angles of the isosceles triangle formed in the second pattern are the same size as those in the zig-zag pattern.
4 **e** The second pattern is the first pattern rotated through a half turn (180°) and with the diagonal line approximately twice as long as the vertical line.
5 **d** The angle between the left vertical side of the square and the diagonal line across the square increases along the sequence. The black shading is always above the diagonal line.
6 **d** The arrow rotates 45° anticlockwise along the sequence; the style of the arrowhead does not change.

7 **e**

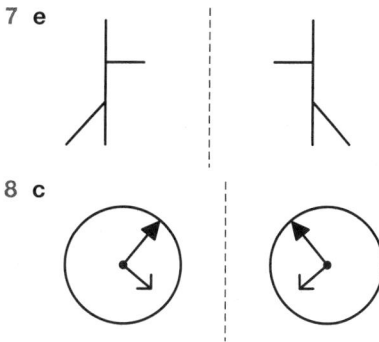

8 **c**

9–10 Even though the explanations below give the letters in order, you may find it easier to identify features linking the second letter and then move on to the first letter.
9 **c** The first letter represents the angle of the thin line at the top (A points up, B horizontal, C points down); the second letter represents the angle of the thick line at the base (X is horizontal, Y points up, Z points down).
10 **e** The first letter represents the angle made by the short line that crosses the vertical line (D small acute/30°, E larger acute/45°, F a right angle/90°); the second letter represents the angle and orientation of the short arrow at the top (L horizontal pointing left, M horizontal pointing right, N diagonal 45° pointing up to the right).

Focus test 12: Number (pages 26–27)

1 **c** All of the shapes on the left have one white circle outside the triangle, two black circles inside, and three white circles across the sides of the triangles.
2 **b** All of the patterns on the left have four lines and three crossing points.
3 **e** Each vertex on the left of the zig-zag in the first shape is represented by a set of three short diagonal lines in the second shape.
4 **e** The second pattern has the same number of white circles and black circles as the number of loops in the first curly line pattern.
5 **c** The number of crosses increases by one along the sequence, with two white circles alternating with one black circle.
6 **d** The number of white circles decreases by one each time along the sequence (so, c or d for 4 circles); the number of circles with a cross increases by one (which could be a, c, d, or e); the number of times the curvy line crosses the side, alternating between the top and the bottom, decreases by one each time (d or e).
7 **e** As the sequence progresses starting top-left, the number of circles is 1–2–3–4–3–2–1–2–3... . The circles alternate between white and black.

Counting up and down the first time, they add in from the top-left up to 4 then decrease from the top-left; counting up and down the second time they add in then decrease from the bottom-right.

8 **d** The patterns in each of the inner four squares of the grid have the same shape as in the square to the left or right of them, and the same number of small shapes as the square above or below them.

9–10 Even though the explanations below give the letters in order, you may find it easier to identify features linking the second letter and then move on to the first letter.

9 **b** The first letter represents the number of circles (A is 3, B is 4, C is 5); the second letter represents the number of small lines at the bottom of the pattern (X is 6, Y is 4, Z is 3).

10 **a** The first letter represents the number of curved lines (A is 1, B is 2, C is 3); the second letter represents the number of sides of the polygon (X is 3, Y is 4, Z is 5).

Focus test 13: Shading (pages 28–29)

1 **d** All of the shapes on the left have cross-hatch shading in the circle.

2 **b** All of the shapes on the left have a black circle inside a circle (dotted/dashed outline) or oval (solid outline) which has diagonal shading with lines from bottom left to top right.

3 **d** The black shaded square of the first pattern becomes a white square in the second pattern and the small square becomes a circle with the diagonal shading rotated by a quarter turn (90°).

4 **b** The first square of the row in the first pattern forms the top-left and bottom-right squares in the second pattern, and the fourth square in the row forms the top-right and bottom-left squares.

5 **e** The shading of circles alternates between a pair of circles with horizontal then vertical lines, and the next pair of circles with 'uphill'/'downhill' diagonal shading. Each pair of circles is separated by a triangle.

6 **c** The shapes follow the repeating sequence –circle–square–triangle– and shading style follows the repeating pattern of –black–horizontal lines–diagonal lines–white–.

7–8 Even though the explanations below give the letters in order, you may find it easier to identify features linking the second letter and then move on to the first letter.

7 **b** The first letter represents the shading style of the quadrilateral (A horizontal lines, B vertical lines, C cross-hatch lines, D diagonal lines); the second letter represents the shading of the irregularly shaped part of the pattern (X is black, Y is cross-hatched lines, Z is diagonal lines).

8 **a** The first letter represents the shading of the triangle (D is diagonal lines, E is black, F is cross-hatch lines); the second letter represents the number of black spots inside the circle (X is 1, Y is 2, Z is 3).

9 **d** Only **d** gives the line-shaded quarter of the face with the X adjacent to the black face.

10 **e** Only **e** gives the face with the small black square adjacent to a face with a white circle with a cross-hatched face adjacent to them both.

Focus test 14: Size (pages 30–31)

1 **c** All of the squares on the left have two circles of equal size on the outside of two corners of the square.

2 **d** All of the patterns on the left are made up of lines of equal lengths to each other.

3 **d** The second shape in each pair is half the height of the first shape.

4 **b** The two small inner shapes in the first pattern increase in size and overlap in the second pattern.

5 **e** The shapes rectangle–square–circle are repeated along the sequence with the rectangles and squares decreasing in size each time and the circles increasing in size.

6 **e** The size of the X decreases for five steps and then increases in size each turn, and the vertical line alternates between long and short.

7–8 Even though the explanations below give the letters in order, you may find it easier to identify features linking the second letter and then move on to the first letter.

7 **c** The first letter represents the size of the black square (X is small, Y is middle sized, Z is large); the second letter represents the length of the arrow (P is short, Q is middle length, R is long). The direction of the arrow is not part of the solution here.

8 **a** The first letter represents the shape and position of the larger shape (A large triangle below small shape, B large circle above small shape, C large triangle below small shape); the second letter represents the shape and position of the smaller shape (X is a small circle on top, Y is a small triangle at the bottom, Z is a small circle at the bottom).

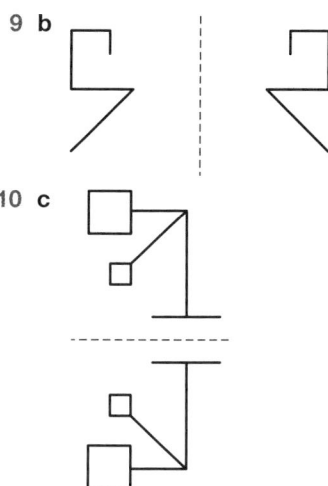

9 b
10 c

9–10 Even though the explanations below give the letters in order, you may find it easier to identify features linking the second letter and then move on to the first letter.

9 c The first letter represents the number of sides of the polygon (A is 6, B is 5, C is 4); the second letter represents the position of the arrow (X is pointing in, Y is pointing out, Z goes across the shape). 1 SHAPE & 2 POSITION

10 b The first letter represents the number of black spots along the line (L is 3, M is 2, N is 1); the second letter represents the size of the circle (M is small, N is middle sized, P is large). 4 NUMBER & 6 SIZE

Mixed paper 1 (pages 34–39)

1 c All of the shapes on the left have curved lines and only diagonal lined shading.
2 d All of the shapes on the left have a black rectangle with two parallel lines, one plain and one dotted, extending from one side.
3 b All of the circles on the left have three of the same shape within them.
4 e All of the patterns on the left are made up of a V-shaped line joining a straight line; the lines of the 'V' are of different lengths and they approximately form a right angle.
5 c All of the circles on the left are the same size and have a straight line extending out of the circle starting from a black spot in the centre.
6 d The first pattern in each pair is rotated through a half turn (180°) to give the second pattern.
7 b The black circle on the top of the first shape becomes white and the black shape below the larger shape also becomes white and moves inside the shape.
8 e In the second pattern the small square increases in size so the black dots now lie on edges of the square. The dots are linked by a curved line, with the same number of white circles as black dots added to the inside of the square.
9 a The second shape is a rhombus with the first shape forming one quarter of it and with the vertically opposite quarter having the same shading.
10 d The second pattern is a repeat of the first with the upper two lines changed from plain lines to dashed lines.
11 c The circle alternates between black and white, the short vertical lines point up or down alternately and progressively move along the horizontal line towards the circle.
12 b The arrows progress anticlockwise by half of a quarter turn (45°) each time.

Focus test 15 (pages 32–33)

1 e All of the shapes on the left have diagonal line shading and a bold dark outline. 5 SHADING
2 a All of the patterns on the left have two crosses and two circles overlapping the outline of the irregular shape. 2 POSITION & 4 NUMBER
3 b Each of the smaller shapes on the outer corners of the first pattern are on the inside of the corresponding corners in the second pattern. 1 SHAPE & 2 POSITION
4 d The same number of lines in the first pattern are in the second pattern, with the first line of the zig-zag in the same orientation as the lines in the first pattern. 2 POSITION & 4 NUMBER
5 d The number of circles decreases by one along the sequence progressively subtracting from the bottom right hand corner up the column, with the shading unaltered. 4 NUMBER & 5 SHADING
6 c The angle of the arrow first increases in a clockwise direction then decreases in an anticlockwise direction, the square alternates between large and small, and the triangle repeating pattern is one large triangle followed by two small ones. 3 ANGLE & 6 SIZE
7 e The shapes in the grid follow a repeating pattern along the rows –triangle with right angle top-left–equilateral triangle pointing up–triangle with right angle top-right–circle–equilateral triangle pointing down–; the shading of the shapes follows the sequence –white–black–diagonal lines–. 1 SHAPE & 5 SHADING
8 d The single shape in the first square of the outer pairs of squares, considered clockwise, is the same shape and shading as those in the adjacent inner grid square. 1 SHAPE & 4 NUMBER

13 **e** The circles alternate with triangles, and the triangles alternate between pointing up or down; the shading of the shapes follows the pattern –horizontal lines–vertical lines–black–.
14 **a** The crosses alternate with black circle shapes, with both the number of crosses and the number of small black circles following the sequence 1–2–3–2–1–.
15 **e** The circles move from right to left along the top line, then progress down to the next horizontal line in the pattern.
16 **d** The first letter represents the shading of the circle (M is white, L has a cross, N is black); the second letter represents the three small shapes (X is triangles, Y is squares, Z is circles).
17 **b** The first letter represents the style of the arrowhead (A is open, B is black arrowhead, C is unshaded arrowhead); the second letter represents the number of lines in the zig-zag (R is 3, T is 4, S is 2).
18 **e** The first letter represents the circles (C is large black, B is large white, A is small black); the second letter represents the number of circles along the line (X is 4, Z is 6, so by deduction Y is 5).
19 **a** The first letter represents the type of triangle (A is an equilateral, B is right-angled, C is a scalene triangle); the second letter represents the number of vertical lines projecting from the triangles (Z is 4, Y is 3, so by deduction X is 2).
20 **b** The first letter represents the style of 'shield' shape (A has a plain white bar across the top, B has an indented bar, C has a vertical division, D has a black bar); the second letter represents the shape inside the 'shield' (L is a white heart, M is small white circle, N is a black circle).
21 **c**
22 **e**
23 **d**

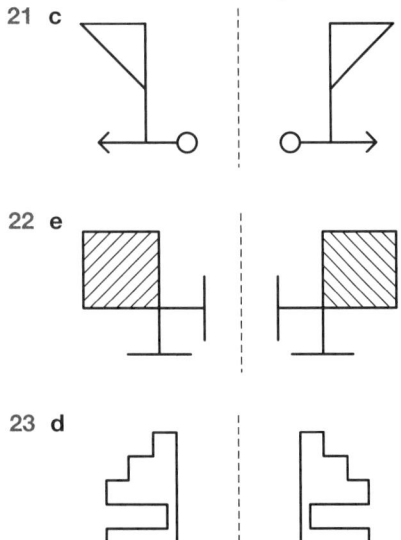

24 **c**

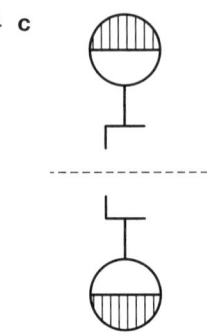

25 **d** Each corner square in the grid is a reflection of the diagonally opposite corner square.
26 **e** The shading style is the same along each row; the pattern of shapes along each row has a heart followed by a square and/or a circle followed by a triangle pointing upwards.
27 **a** The shape in the outer rectangles is a reflection of the shape on the opposite side of the inner square.
28 **e** The shape in the outer corner of the outer triangles is the same as the shape that is opposite in the middle triangle.
29 **d** The arrow points away from a white circle (**a**, **b** or **d**) and the point of the heart shape is adjacent to the edge of the circle face.
30 **a** The black headed arrow points to the face with the black circle.
31 **c** The V-shape points to the face with an X (**c** or **d**) and is adjacent to a face with a square.
32 **b** The two faces with diagonal lines share an edge (**b** or **e**) and both are adjacent to the face with a black circle.
33 **c**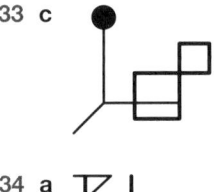
34 **a**
35 **b**
36 **c**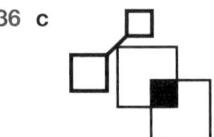

Mixed paper 2 (pages 40–45)

1. **d** All of the shapes on the left have a right-angled triangle and a circle overlapping the outline of the triangle.
2. **e** All of the shapes on the left are curly arrows with three loops along the line.
3. **b** All of the shapes on the left are irregular dark grey shapes with one circle within them.
4. **a** All of the shapes on the left are made up of three zig-zag lines with a white circle on the middle line of the three.
5. **c** All of the shapes on the left are made up of a square, a circle and a triangle.
6. **e** The second shape of the pair is a square with the same number of X crosses in it as there are circles within the rectangle of the first shape.
7. **c** The second shape is the first shape within a white square, adjacent to another square where the shading of the parts in the first square are reversed.
8. **a** The second shape is a repeat of the first shape surrounded by a white 'frame' of the same shape.
9. **e** The second shape has the same number of lines and crossing points as there are lines in the zig-zag of the first shape.
10. **d** The circle in the first shape of the pair has become a quadrilateral with the same shading pattern.
11. **c** The sequence is made up of square coils; they alternate between coils that are increasing and coils that are decreasing by one line at a time.
12. **b** The vertical pattern alternates with the rows of three circles; it increases in length with a shape added at the bottom each time.
13. **c** The circle at the tip of the triangles which point down follows a repeated shading pattern of lined–black–white–; the alternating triangles have circles within them which follow the same shading sequence starting with black.
14. **e** The sequence grows with the addition of shapes or lines at the top of the vertical line, which is then copied at the bottom of the line in the next pattern.
15. **d** The number of straight lines in the shapes decreases by one each time and the circle alternates between black and white.
16. **c** The first letter represents the shape of the cylinder (A with a bend, B narrow, C wide); the second letter represents the pattern on the side of the cylinder (X is cross-hatched lines, Y is black and white stripes, so by deduction Z is white bands).
17. **b** The first letter represents the outer shape (P is a small square, Q a vertically orientated rectangle, R a horizontally orientated rectangle, S a large square); the second letter represents the number of circles in the shape (X is 3, Y is 2, Z is 1).
18. **d** The first letter represents the orientation of the square U-shape (A open on the left, B open on the right, C open at the base, so by deduction D open at the top); the second letter represents the number of wavy lines crossing the U-shape (L is 1, M is 2, N is 3).
19. **a** The first letter represents the outer shape (D a heart, E a 'flower' with 7 petals, F a 'flower' with 5 petals); the second letter represents the shading of the circle (X is white, Y is lines, Z is black).
20. **b** The first letter represents the line style at the bottom of the shape (E a single wavy line, F a zig-zag line, G a double wavy line, H a dotted line); the second letter represents the number of squares projecting on the top of the rectangle (L is 1, M is 2, N is 3).
21. **c**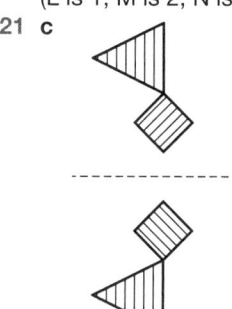
22. **d**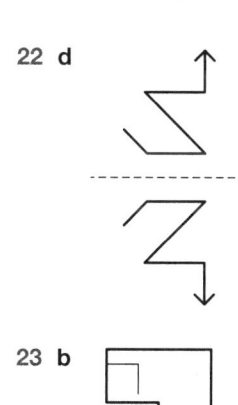
23. **b**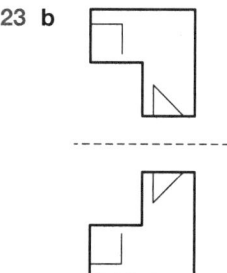

24 a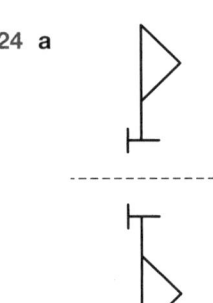

25 **d** The spots move diagonally repeating from top-left to centre to bottom-right along the squares in any one row and continuing onto the next row.
26 **a** The circles in the outer triangles have the same shading as the opposite small triangles within the central triangle.
27 **e** The right-angled triangle rotates a quarter turn (90°) clockwise along the row and then onto the next row; the circles along each row of the grid are black–white–black.
28 **e** The white shapes in the central squares are the same as the white shapes in the corresponding outer rectangles.
29 **d** A face with a single arrowhead points to the bottom of a smiley face (**c** or **d**) and has a white circle adjacent to the smiley face.
30 **b** The face with the double ended arrow is adjacent to the face with the quarter-shaded X but not pointing at it.
31 **e** The face with lines has them parallel to the line of symmetry of the U-shape (**a** or **e**) and is adjacent to a face with a white circle.
32 **c** The base of the white triangle is adjacent to the black face (**a**, **c** or **e**) and adjacent to (not pointing to) a face with plain lines.
33 e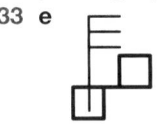
34 c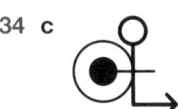
35 d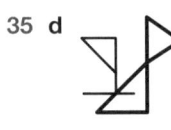
36 a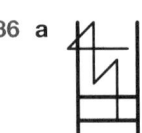

Mixed paper 3 (pages 46–51)

1 **e** All of the shapes on the left have a straight dashed line crossing them with a black circle at one end of the line.
2 **b** All of the shapes on the left have a regular 2-D shape within an irregular one, with one part shaded with diagonal lines and the other part shaded black.
3 **c** All of the patterns on the left are made up of five straight lines connected in an irregular zig-zag pattern.
4 **d** All of the shapes on the left are made up of two overlapping white squares.
5 **a** All of the shapes on the left have an arrow from the edge of the shape pointing diagonally to the top-right.
6 **c** The triangle in the first shape becomes a square in the second shape, and the circle becomes a pentagon.
7 **e** The large square becomes a rectangle, the black spot moves to the vertically opposite corner inside the shape, and the inner white shape moves to the vertically opposite corner outside the rectangle.
8 **a** The wide angle of the first shape is reduced to an acute angle and line shading becomes cross-hatched shading in the second shape.
9 **d** The line of spots rotates through a quarter turn (90°) and each spot is 'covered' by a semi-circle.
10 **b** The shading in the first vertical section of the shape moves to the middle section and the circle at the top of the third section moves from top to bottom.
11 **e** The middle-sized pattern in the sequence alternates with the tall pattern and the short one along the sequence.
12 **d** The shapes follow the repeating pattern of large triangle–large circle–middle sized circle–small circle–small triangle; diagonal line shading alternates with black shading.
13 **c** The number of short straight lines crossing the single line decreases by one each time along the sequence and the short lines do not touch each other.
14 **c** The polygons alternate with the zig-zag patterns and the number of sides/lines in the shapes deceases by one progressively with each pair along the sequence.
15 **d** The small circle is rotating clockwise by half of a quarter turn (45°) each time around the inside of the large circle. Its colour alternates between white and black.

16 **c** The first letter represents the outer shape (A is a triangle, B a circle, C a square); the second letter represents the inner shape (X is a square, Y a triangle, so by deduction Z is a circle).

17 **b** The first letter represents the position of the short diagonal line (A the top-left corner, B the bottom-right corner, C the bottom-left corner); the second letter represents the shading of the inner circle (X is black, Y has a cross, Z is white).

18 **e** The first letter represents the number of circles (A is 3, B is 4, C is 5); the second letter represents the other shape within the pattern (X is a triangle, Y a quadrilateral, Z a pentagon).

19 **b** The first letter represents the shading of the square (A is diagonal lines, B cross-hatched lines, C is black, D is white); the second letter represents the position of the triangle in relation to the square (P is below, Q is above, R is to the right, so by deduction S is to the left).

20 **d** The first letter represents the line-style of the circle (D is a single line, E is a double line with one solid and one dotted line, F is a double solid line); the second letter represents the style of the arrow (X is an arrow with an angle along it, Y is a straight arrow, Z is a wavy arrow).

21 **d**

22 **b**

23 **e**

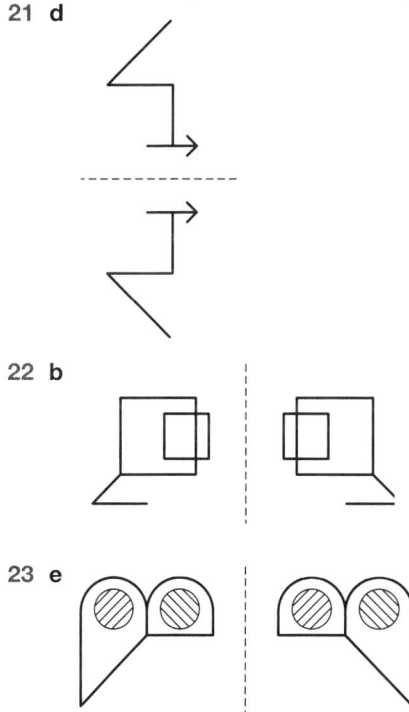

24 **c**

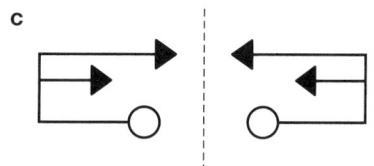

25 **a** The patterns along the bottom row of the grid are the same as those in the top row but with a black circle.

26 **e** The circle is in the outer rectangles in the same relative position each time and copies the shading of the adjacent inner small square.

27 **c** The patterns in the outer rectangles are the second and third shapes of the adjacent inner square, considered moving clockwise around the shape.

28 **b** The outer corner of the outer triangles takes the pattern from the opposite corner of the inner triangle.

29 **d** The top edge of the heart must be adjacent to a face with a white circle.

30 **e** Three plain single arrows must all point to one of the vertices.

31 **c** The side of the smiley face must be adjacent to the black triangle.

32 **b** The tip of a white triangle and the tip of a black triangle must point towards the face with the X (b, c or e) and be adjacent to each other.

33 **d**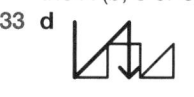

34 **e**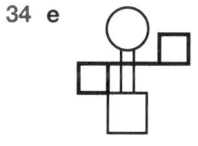

35 **c**

36 **a**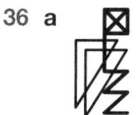

NOTES

Which one completes the sequence? Circle the letter.

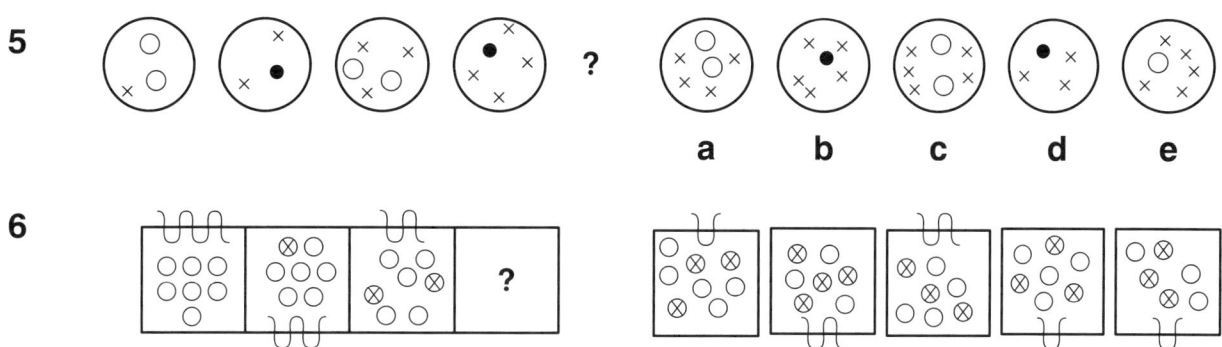

Which one completes the grid? Circle the letter.

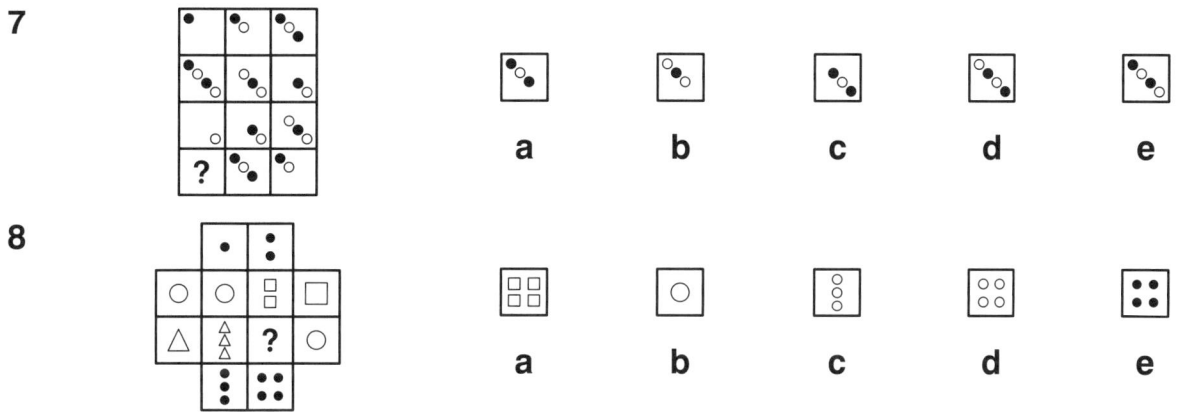

Which code matches the last shape? Circle the letter.

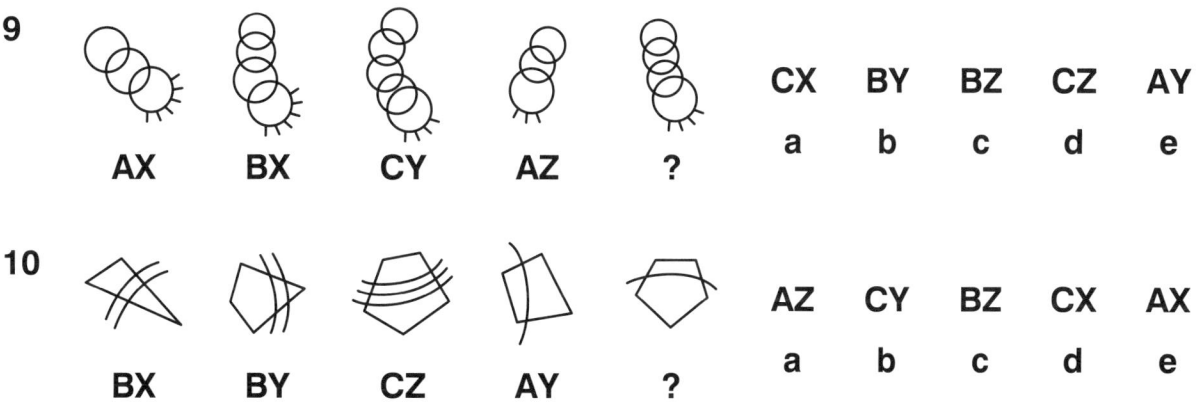

Focus test 13 — Shading

The type of SHADING in all or part of a pattern may be significant, so look carefully at any shading used. It may be a key feature on its own or it may be part of a more complex pattern, for example, by being combined with a SHAPE or NUMBER pattern.

Which one belongs to the group on the left? Circle the letter.

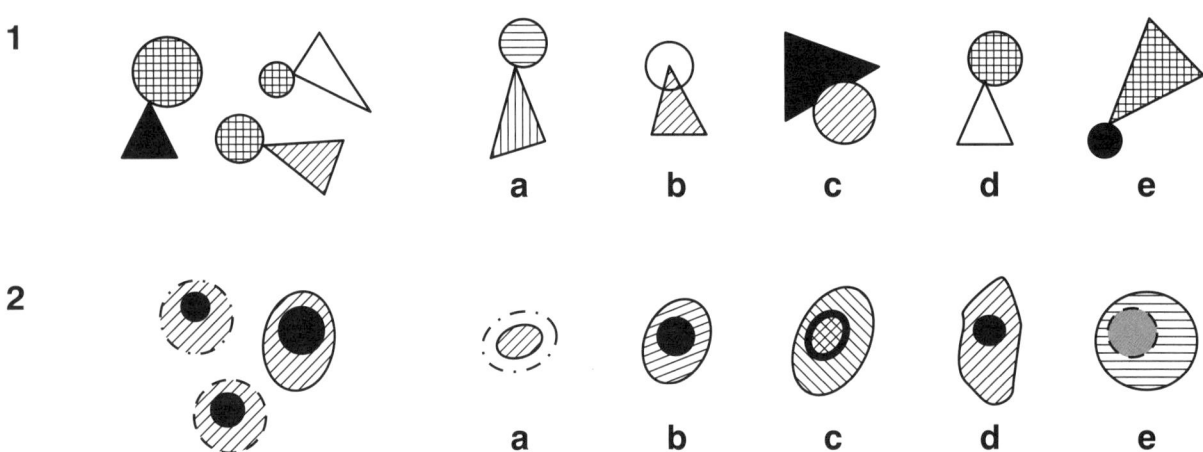

Which one completes the second pair in the same way as the first pair? Circle the letter.

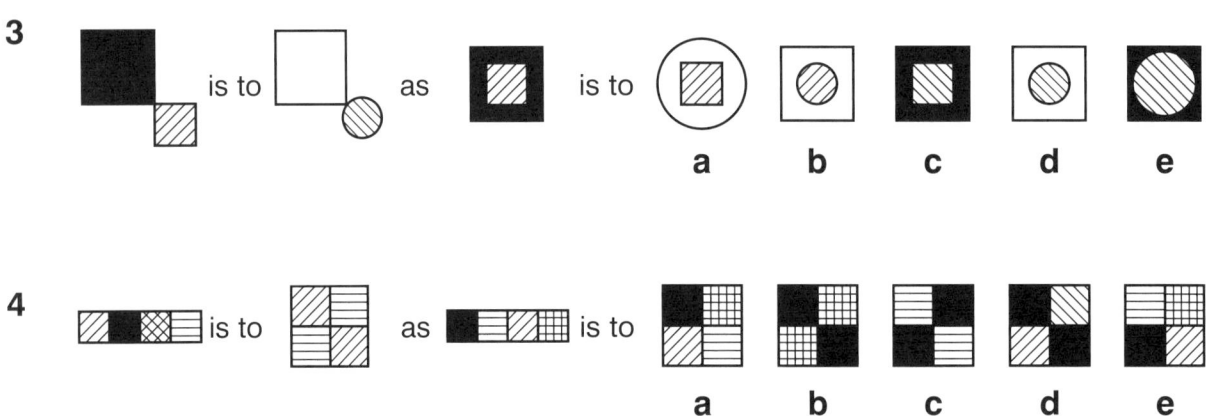

Which one completes the sequence? Circle the letter.

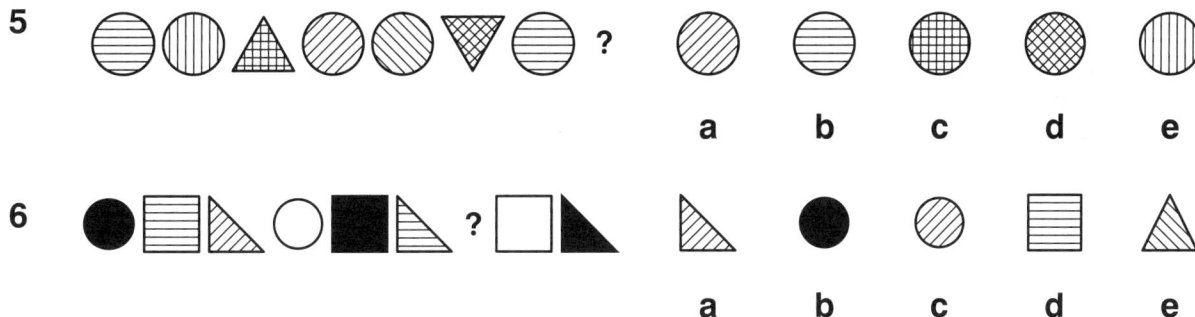

Which code matches the last shape? Circle the letter.

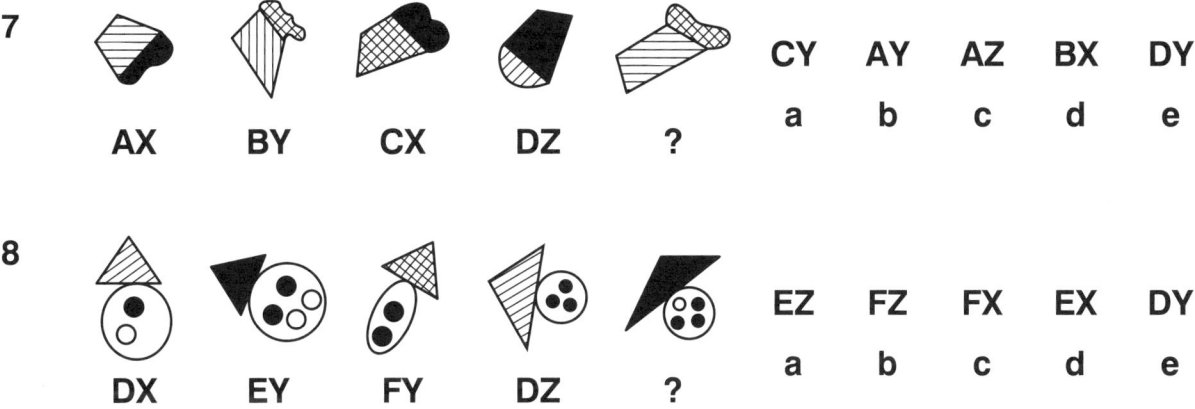

Which of these nets will fold to give the cube on the left? Circle the letter.

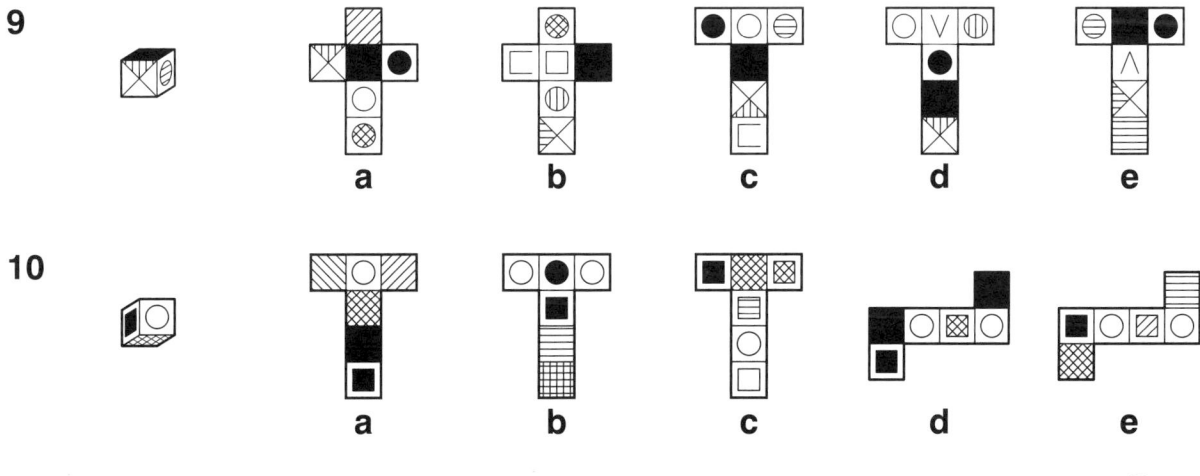

Focus test 14 — Size

> It is very important to notice the SIZE of different shapes and line lengths since small variations in these may need to be identified to find the correct answer.

Which one belongs to the group on the left? Circle the letter.

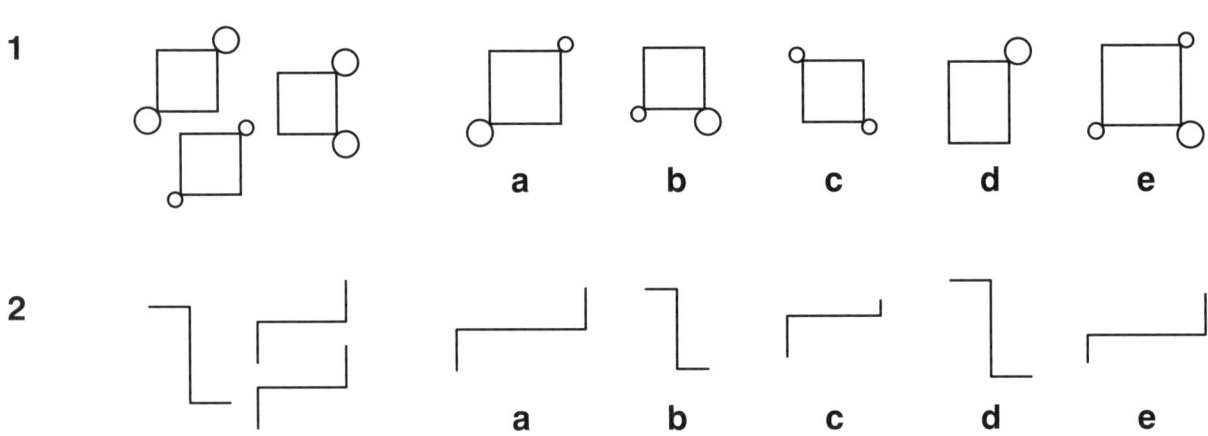

Which one completes the second pair in the same way as the first pair? Circle the letter.

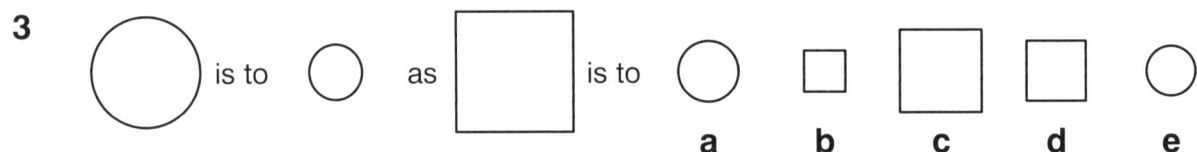

> When a shape is irregular, exact size cannot be compared so easily, but the size of one part of the pattern relative to another part may be significant.

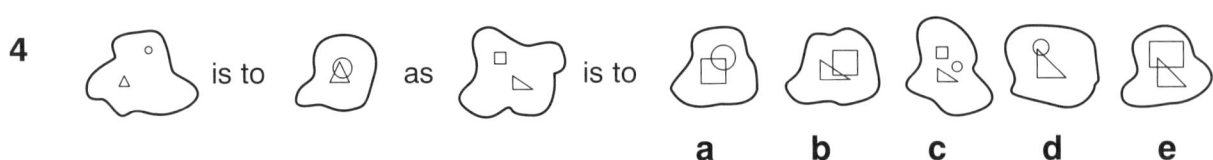

Which one completes the sequence? Circle the letter.

5

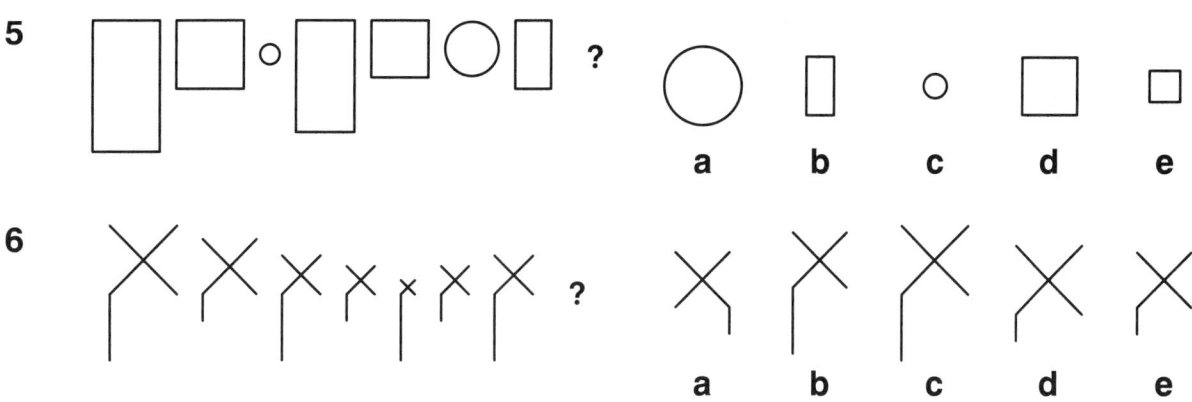

6

Which code matches the last shape? Circle the letter.

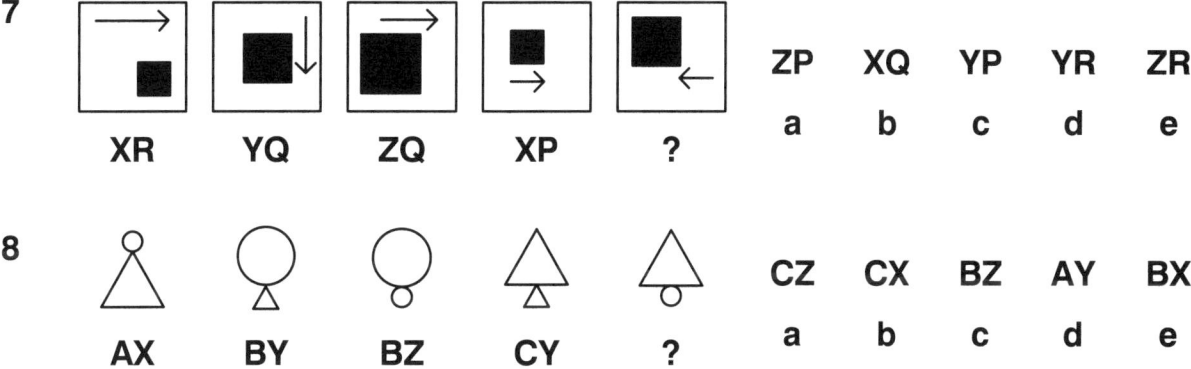

Which one is a reflection of the pattern on the left? Circle the letter.

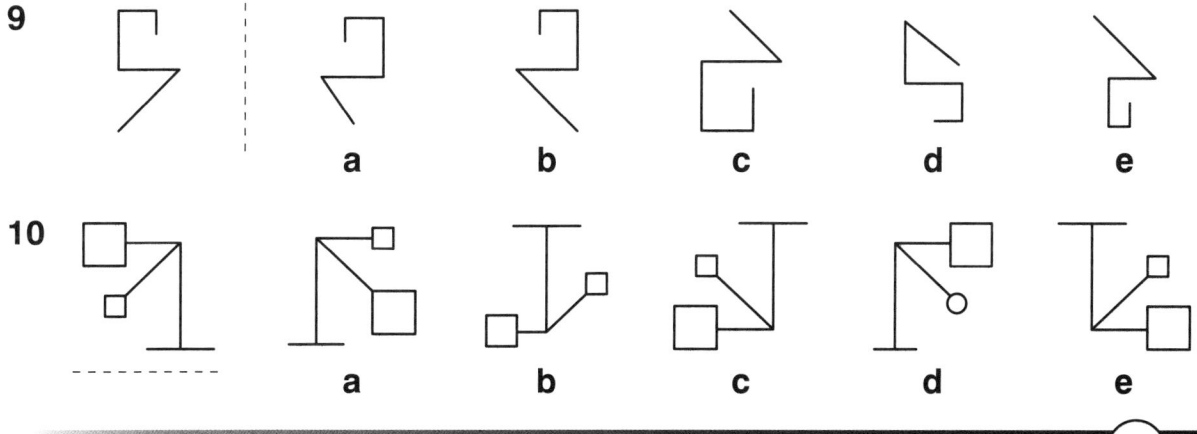

Focus test 15

As well as working out the answers, see if you can also identify the key characteristics that you should notice for each question (there may be more than one). Circle the numbers of all relevant key characteristics.

Which one belongs to the group on the left? Circle the letter.

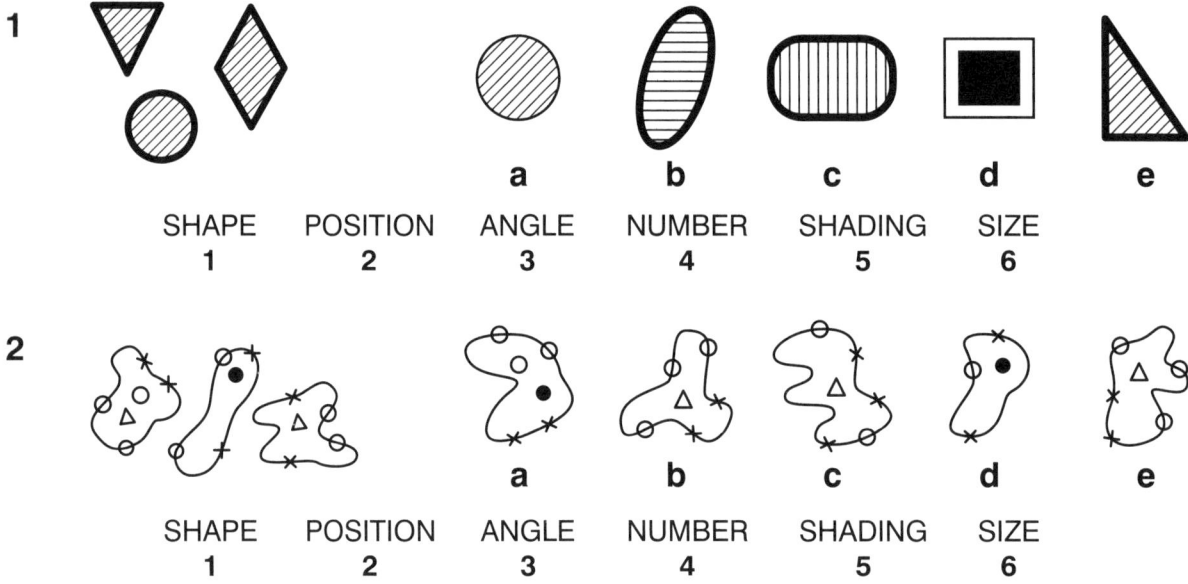

Which one completes the second pair in the same way as the first pair? Circle the letter.

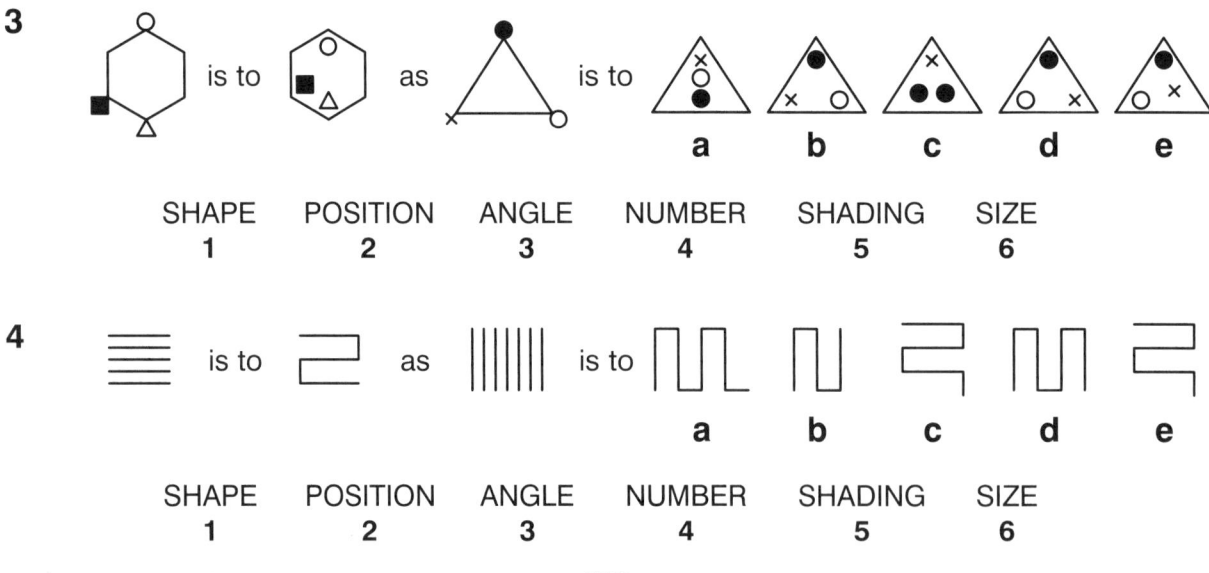

Which one completes the sequence? Circle the letter.

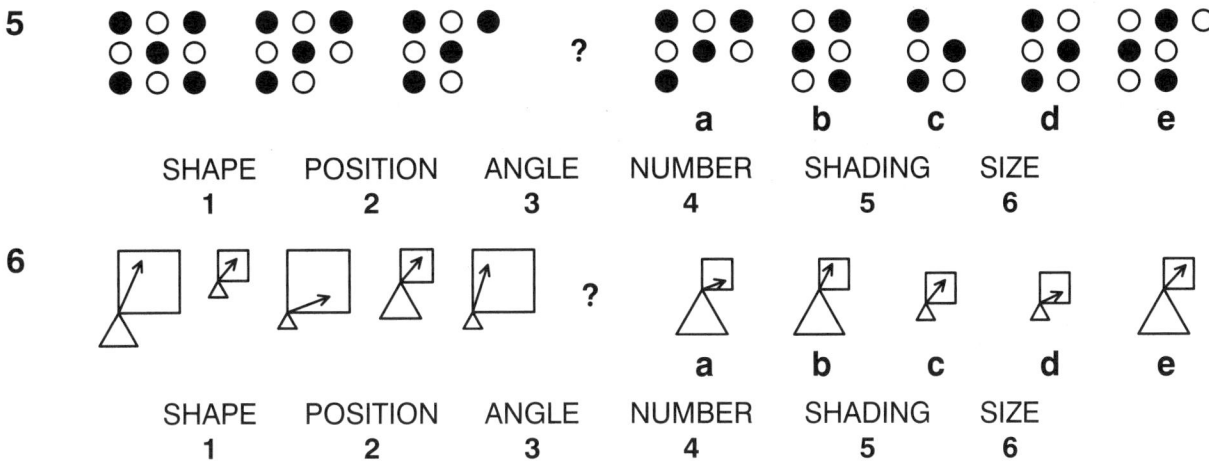

Which one completes the grid? Circle the letter.

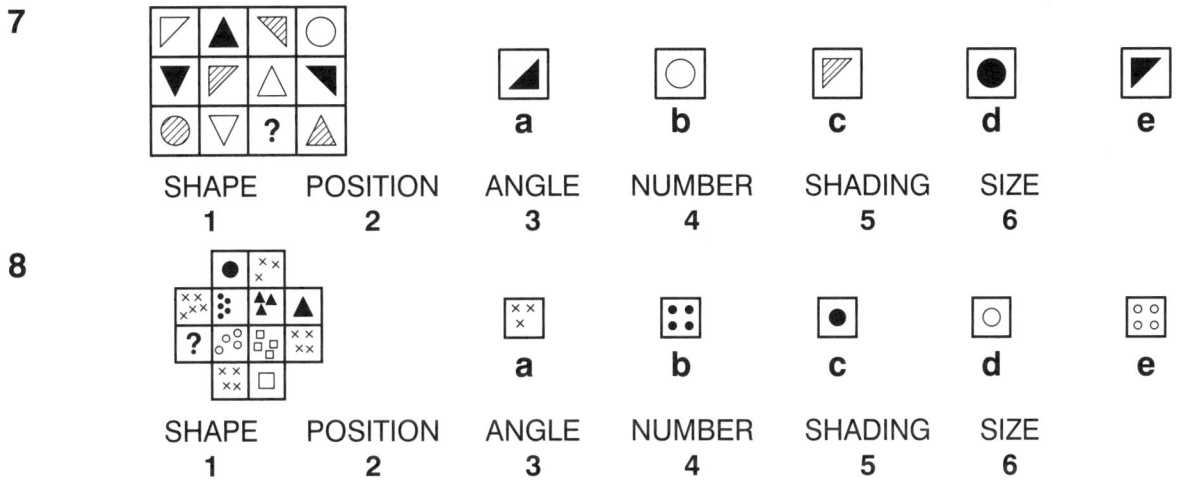

Which code matches the last shape? Circle the letter.

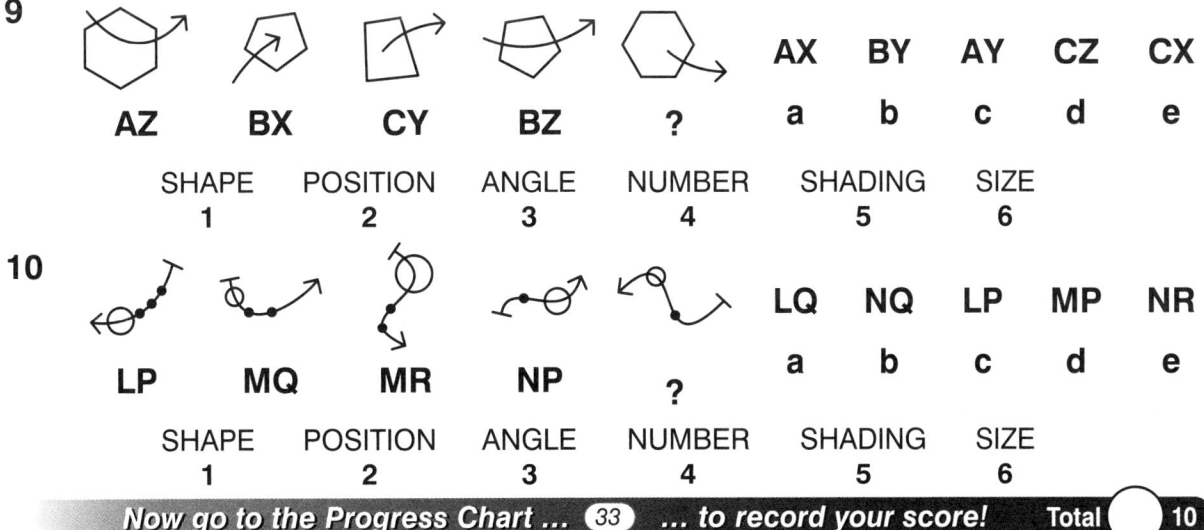

Now go to the Progress Chart ... 33 ... to record your score!   Total   10

Mixed paper 1

Which one belongs to the group on the left? Circle the letter.

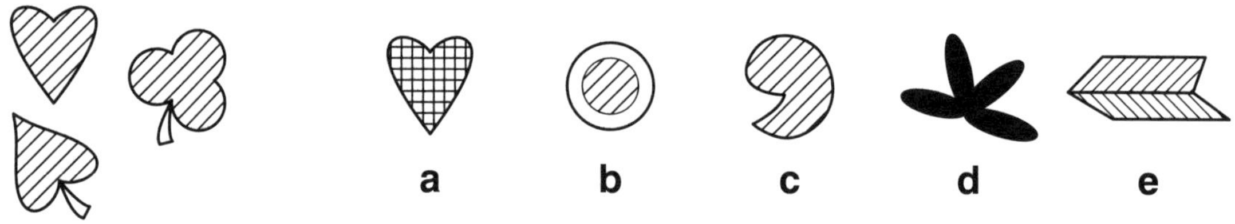

Example

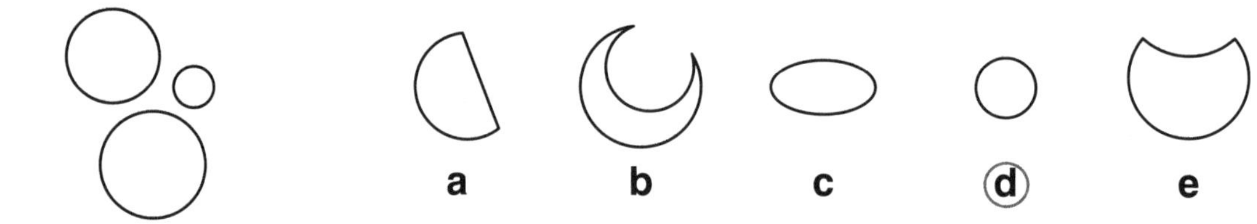

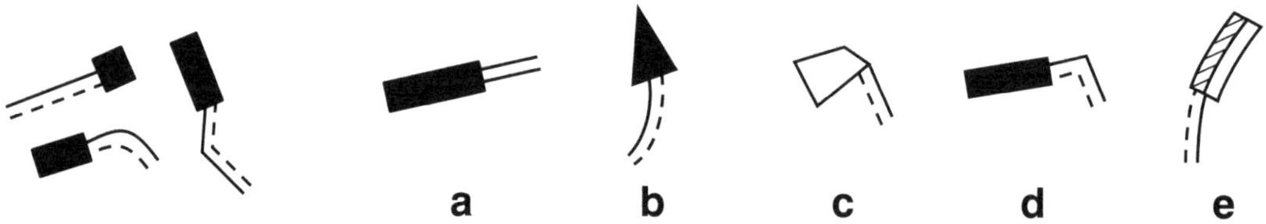

1.
2.
3.
4.
5.

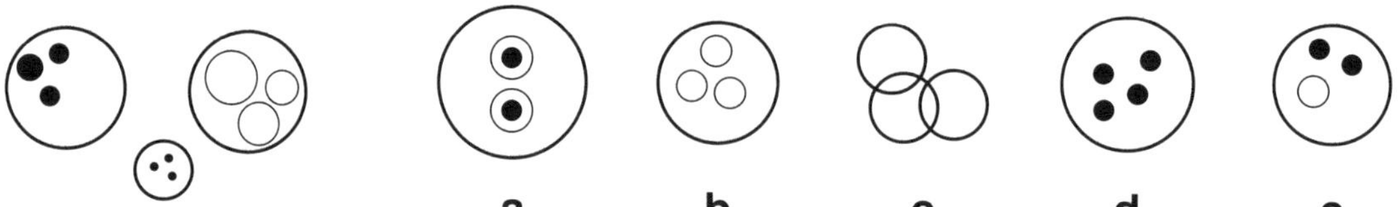

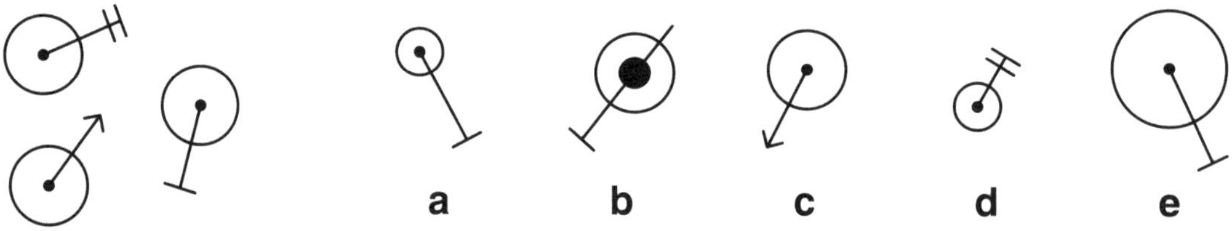

Which one completes the second pair in the same way as the first pair? Circle the letter.

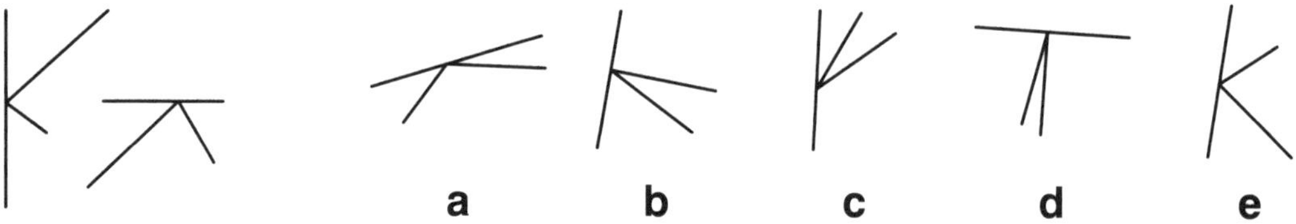

Example

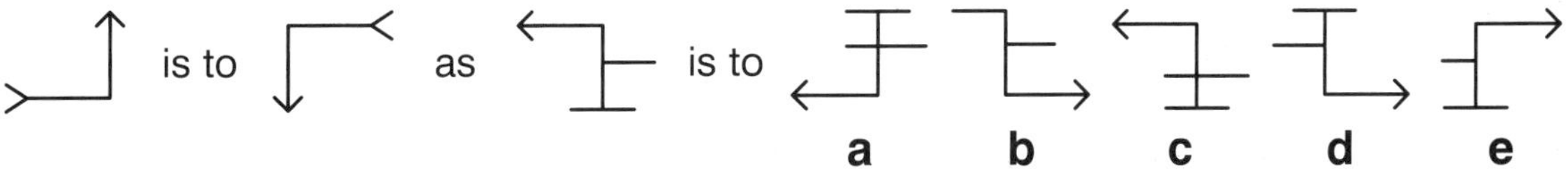

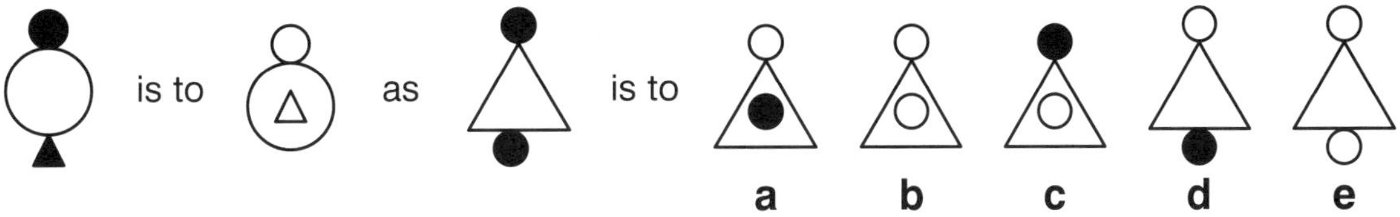

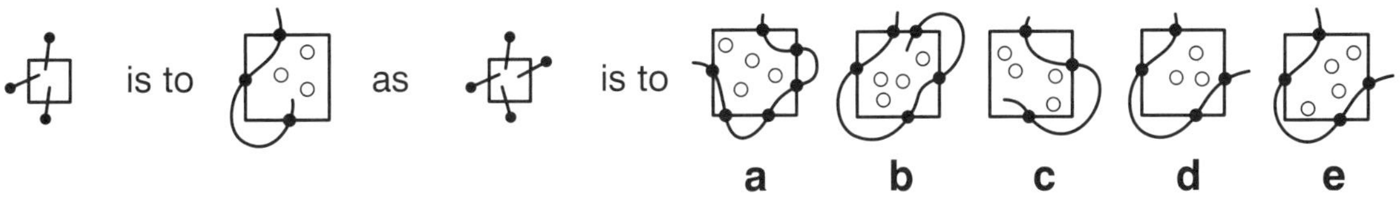

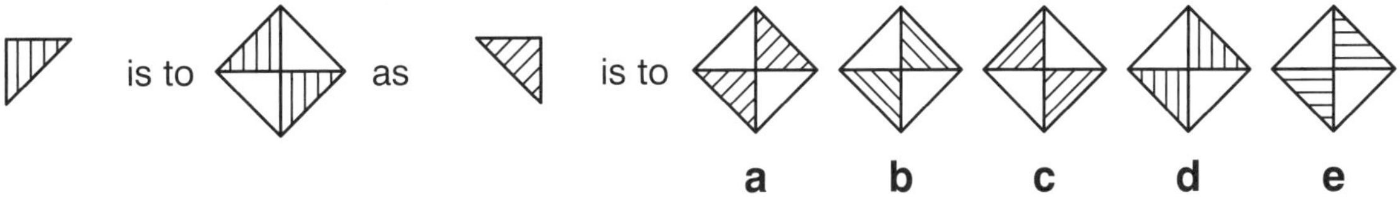

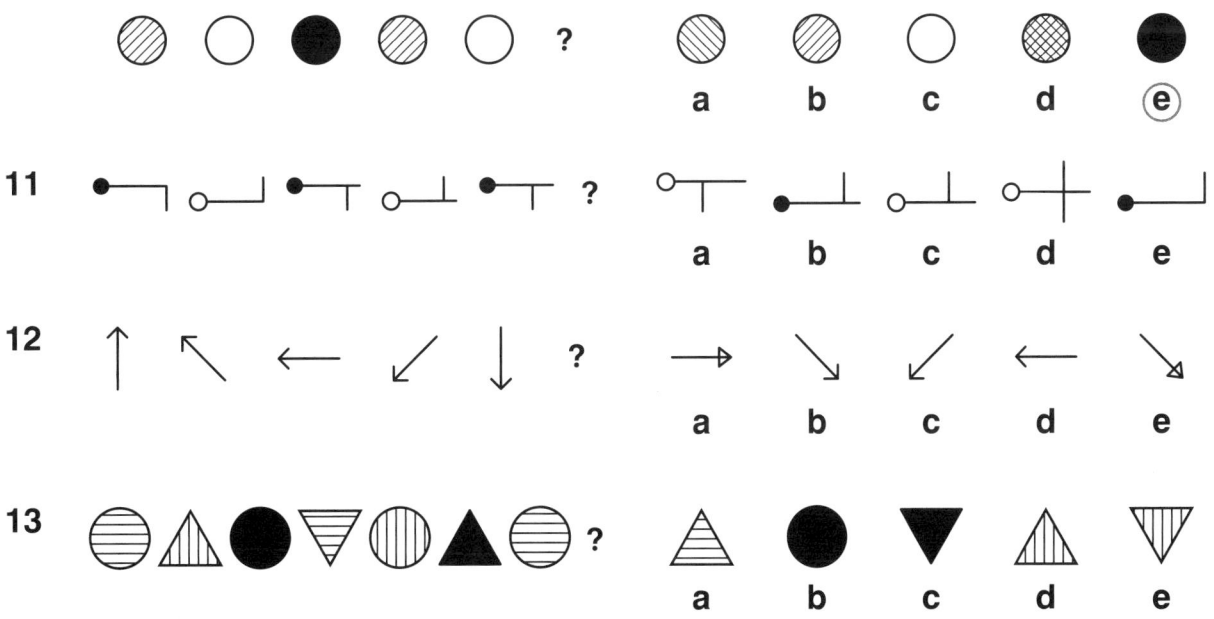

14

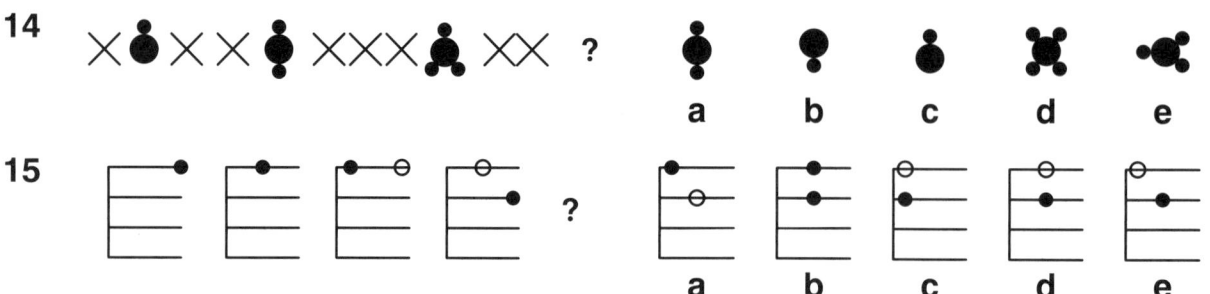

a	b	c	d	e

15

a	b	c	d	e

Which code matches the last shape? Circle the letter.

Example

AY	CX	BZ	CZ	AZ
a	b	(c)	d	e

16

NY	LX	MZ	MY	NZ
a	b	c	d	e

17

AT	CT	AS	BS	CR
a	b	c	d	e

18

CY	BY	AX	CZ	AY
a	b	c	d	e

19

BX	BZ	AX	CX	CZ
a	b	c	d	e

20

DL	BN	AM	CN	BM
a	b	c	d	e

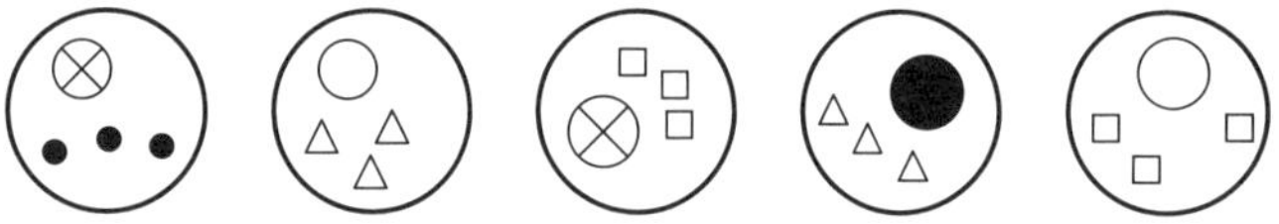

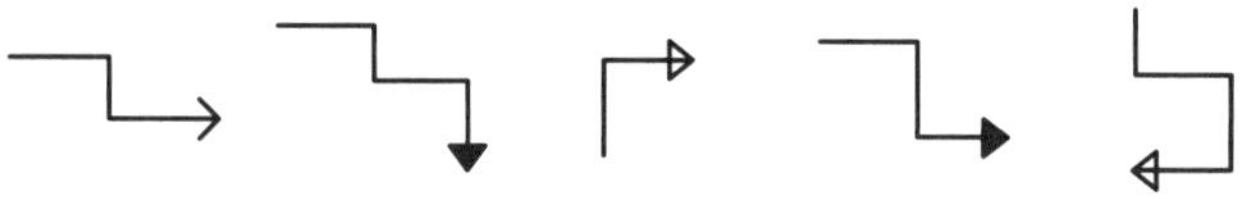

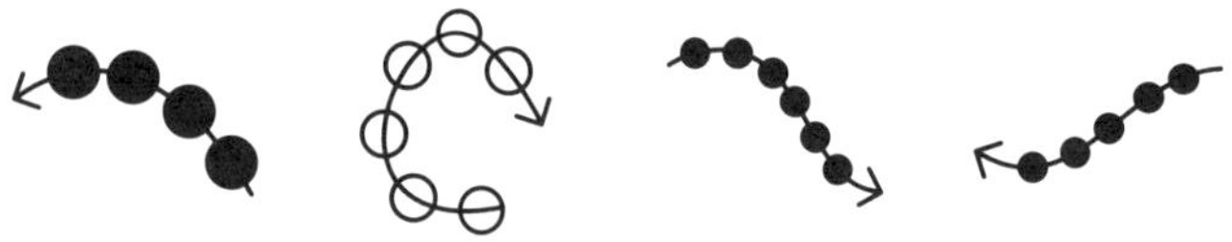

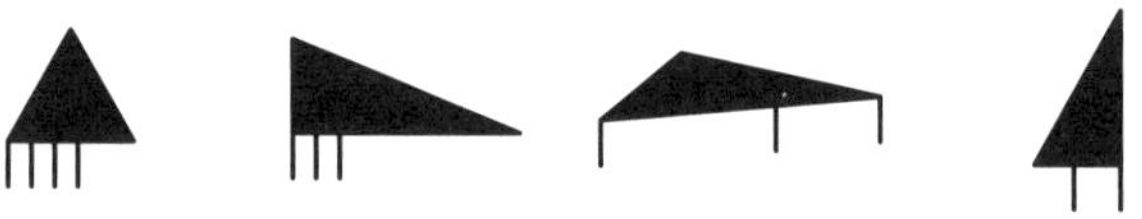

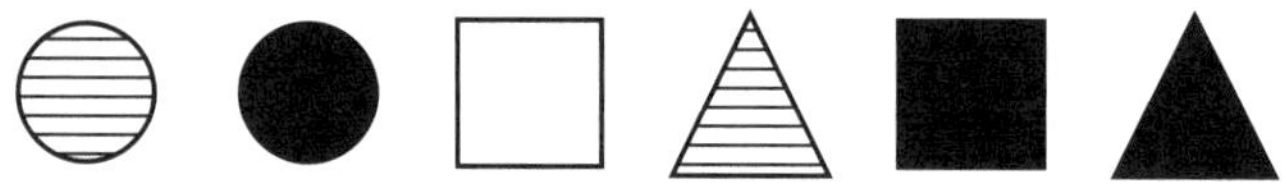

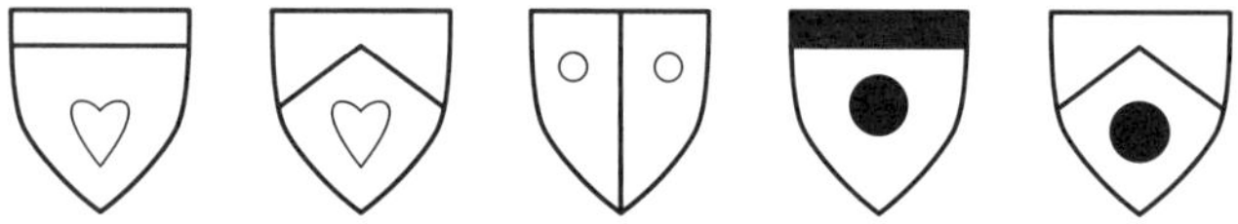

Which one is a reflection of the pattern on the left? Circle the letter.

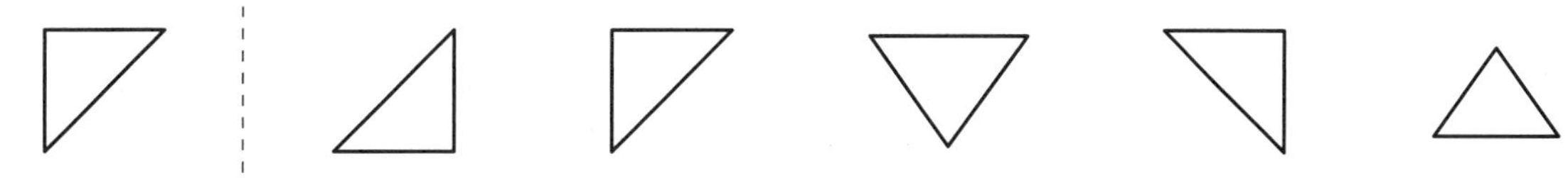

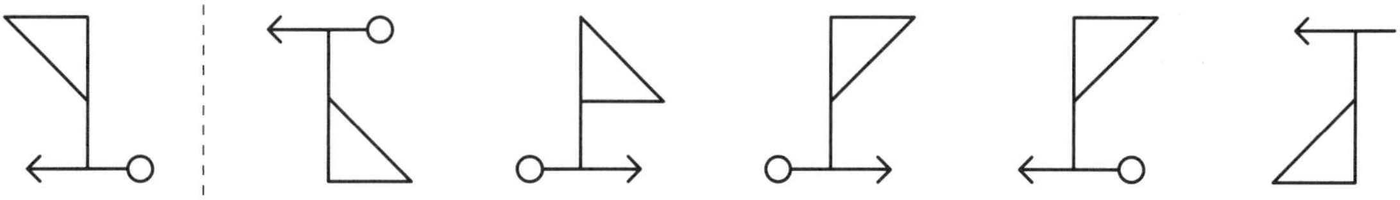

Example

a b c d e

21

a b c d e

22

a b c d e

23

a b c d e

24

a b c d e

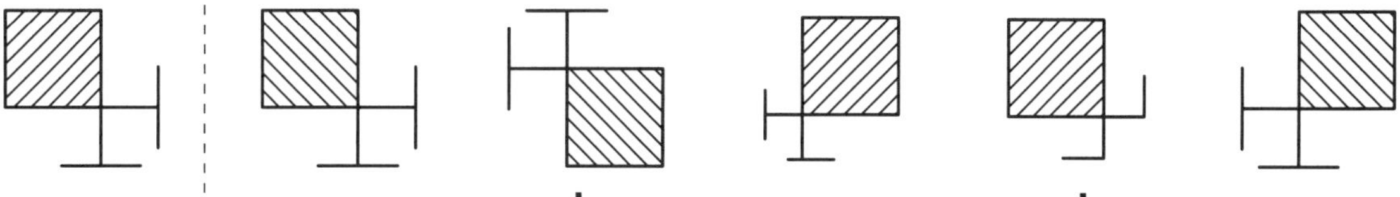

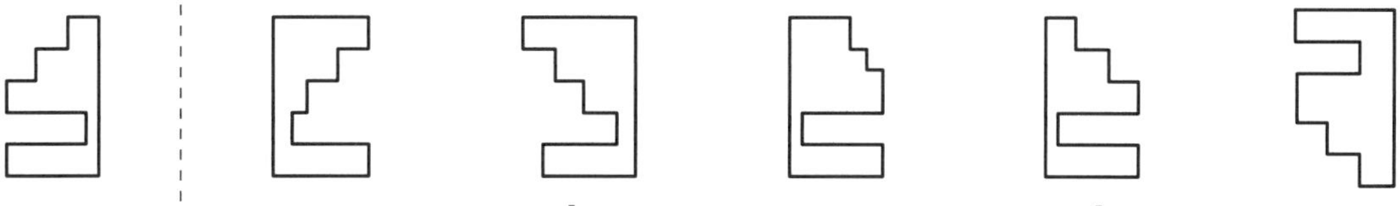

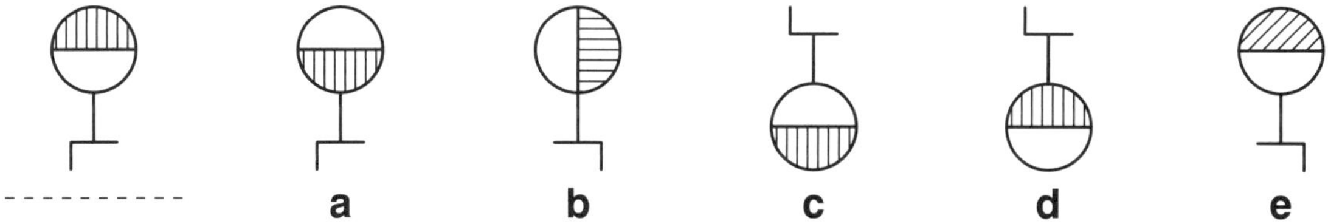

Which one completes the grid? Circle the letter.

Example

a b c d e

25

a b c d e

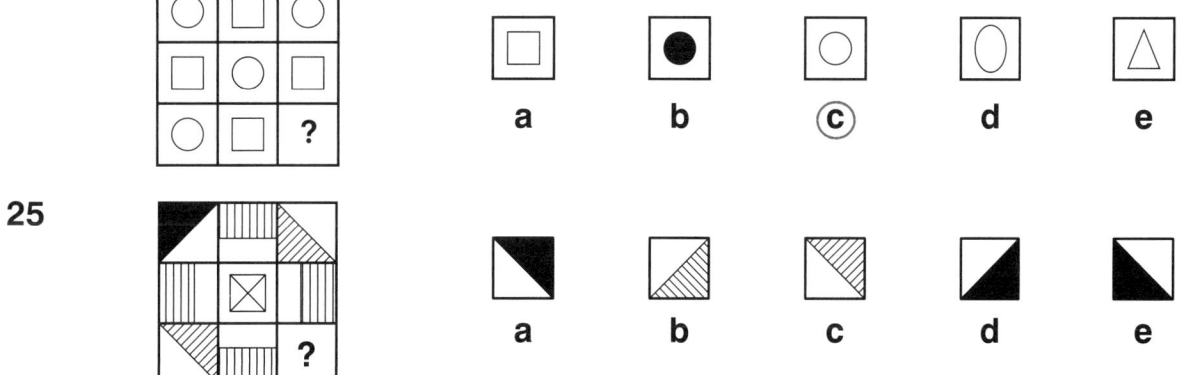

26

27

28

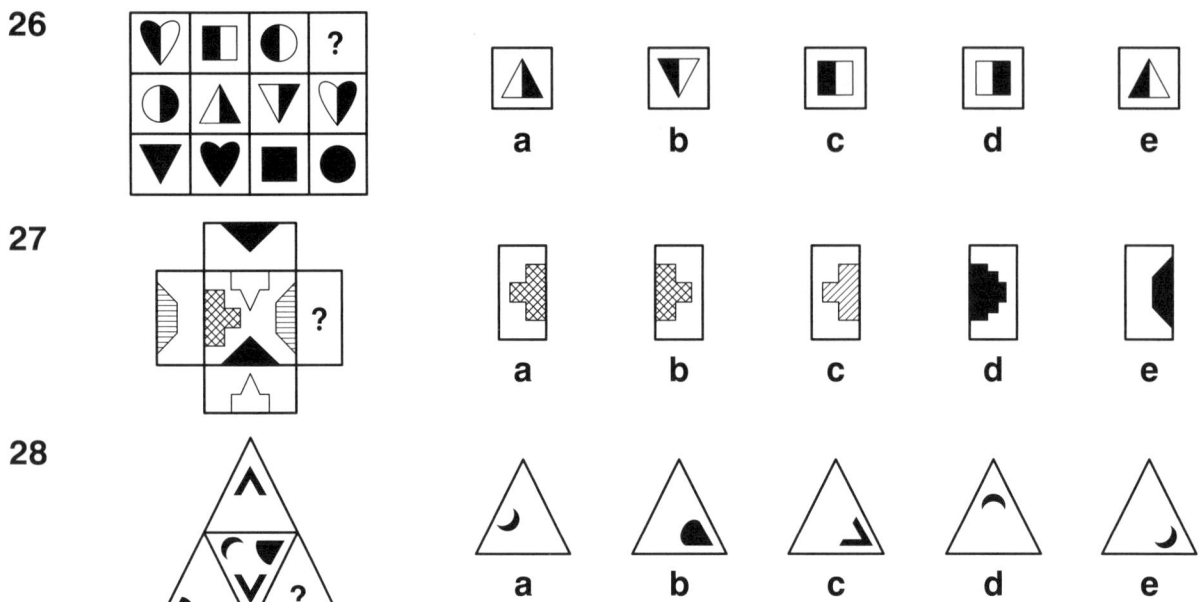

Which of these nets will fold to give the cube on the left? Circle the letter.

Example

29

30

31

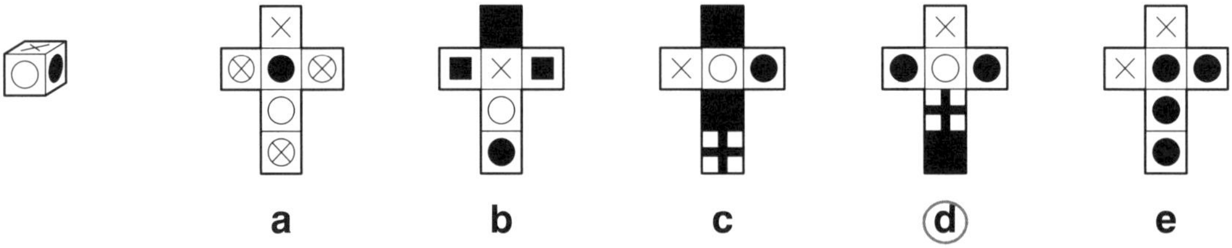

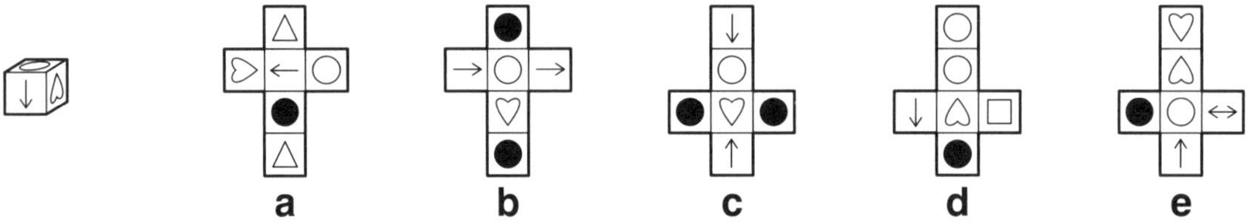

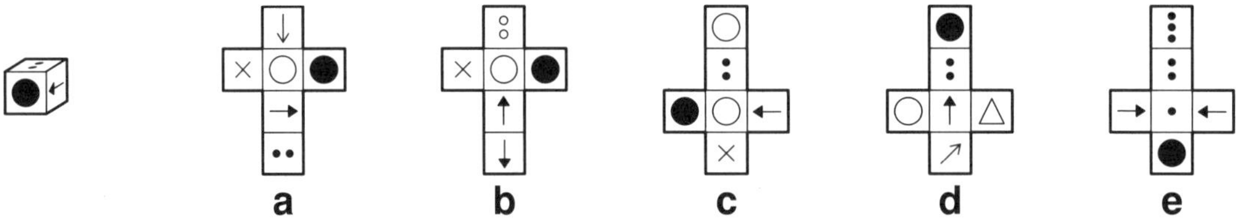

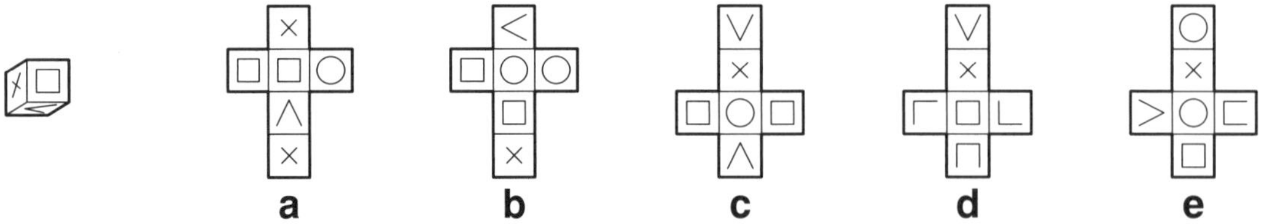

32

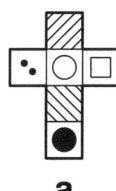

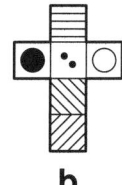

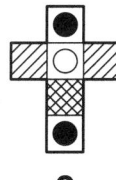

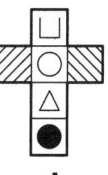

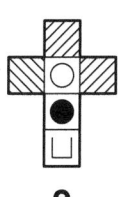

a b c d e

Which pattern is made by combining the two shapes on the left?
Circle the letter.

Example

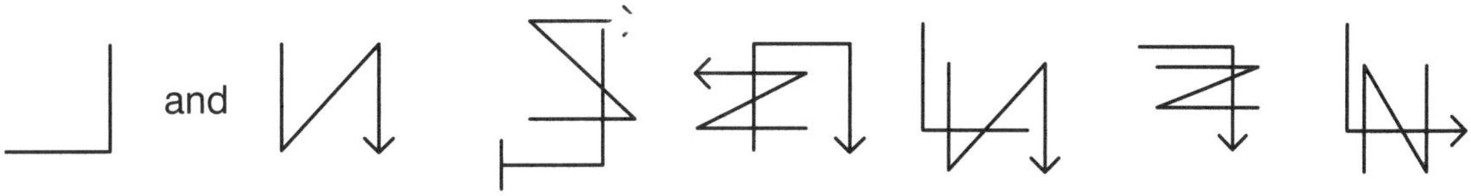

a b (c) d e

33

a b c d e

34

a b c d e

35

a b c d e

36

a b c d e

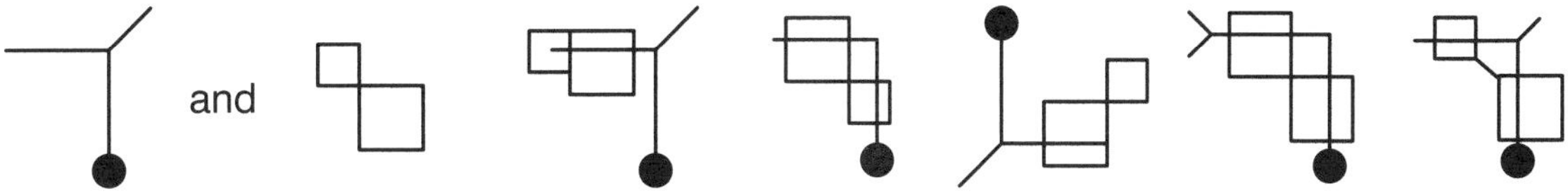

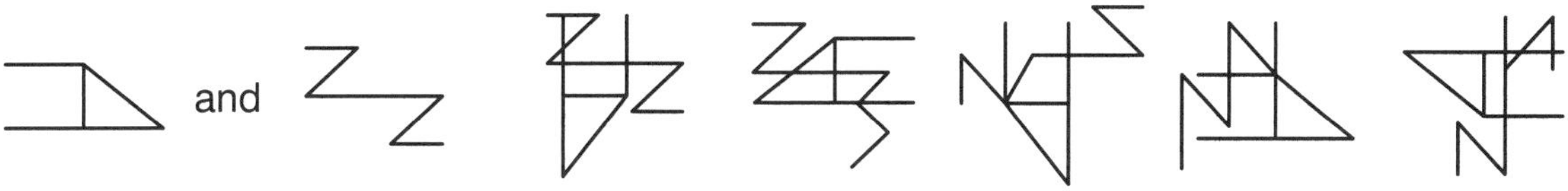

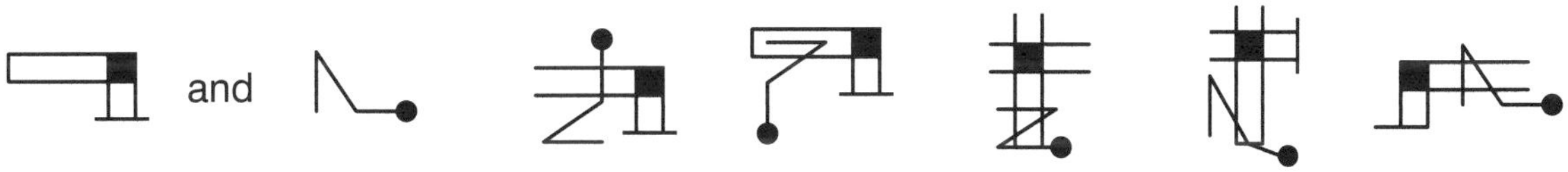

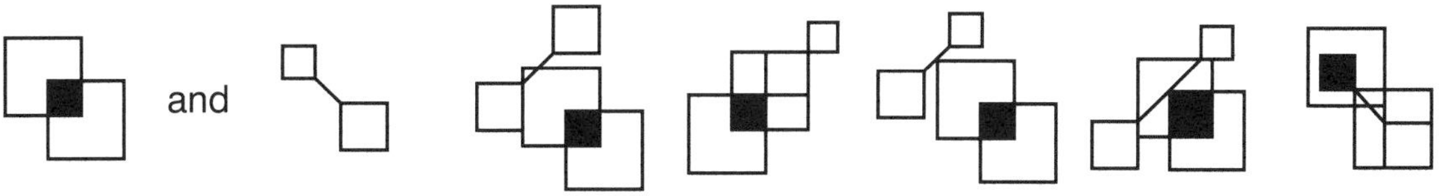

Now go to the Progress Chart … 39 … to record your score! Total [ ] 36

Mixed paper 2

Which one belongs to the group on the left? Circle the letter.

Example

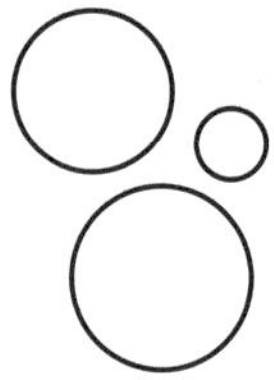

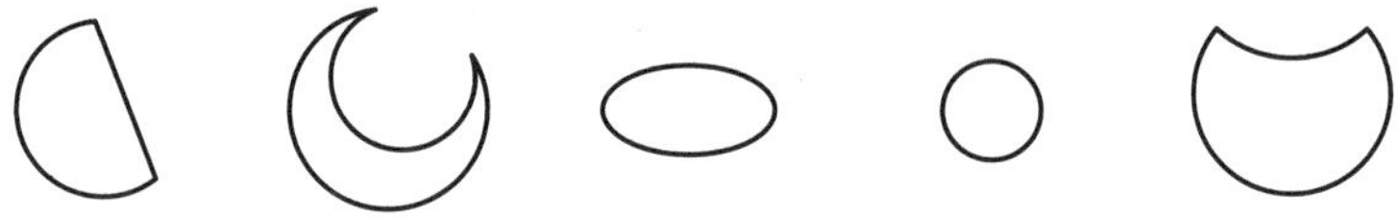

a b c (d) e

1

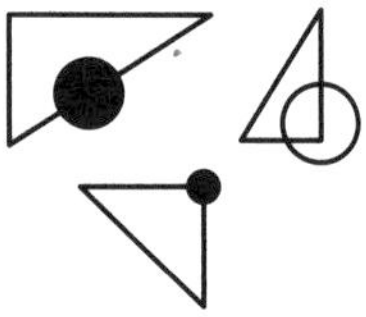

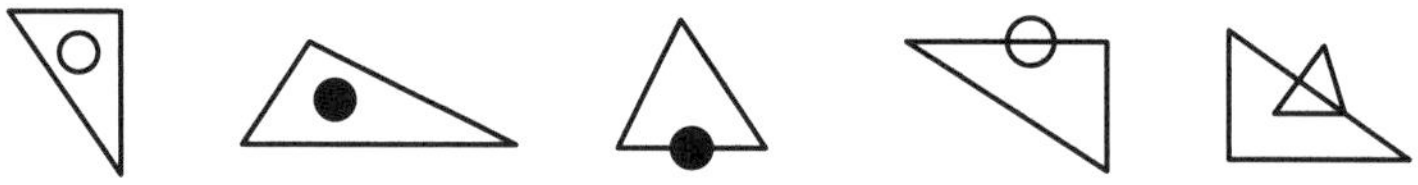

a b c d e

2

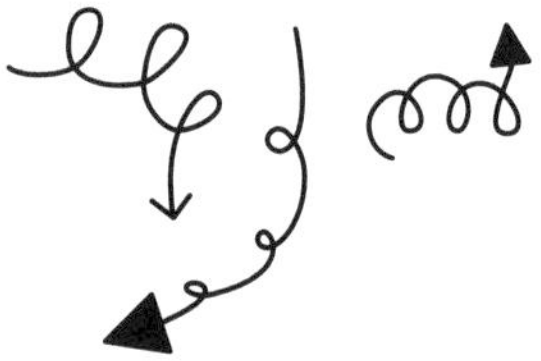

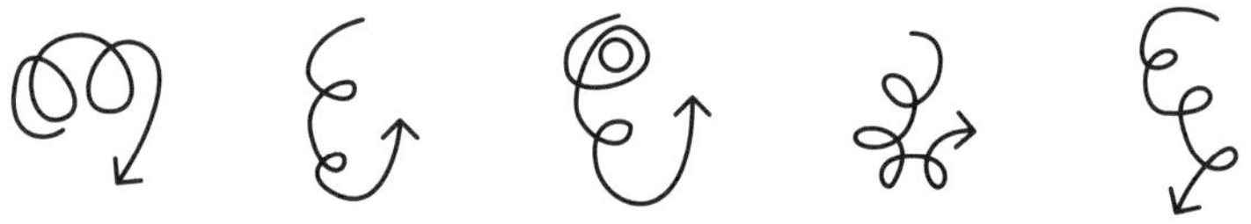

a b c d e

3

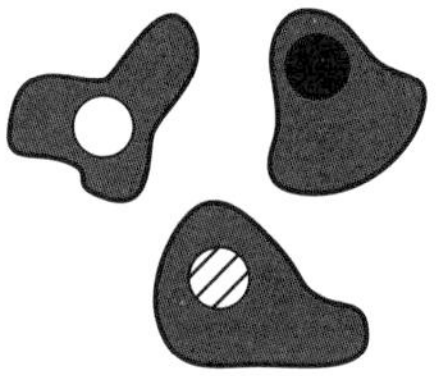

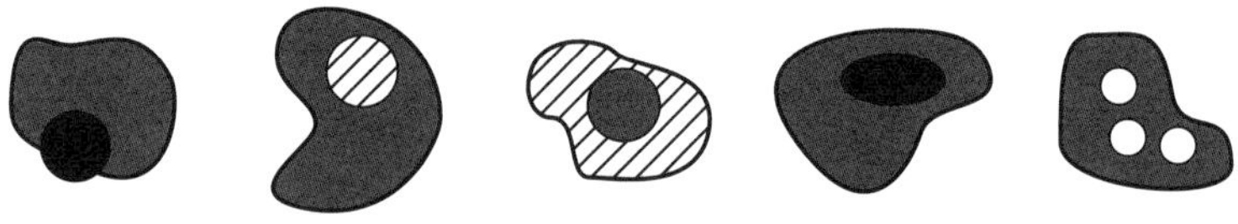

a b c d e

4

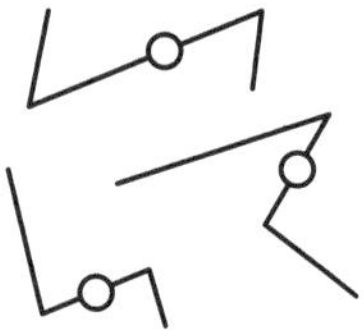

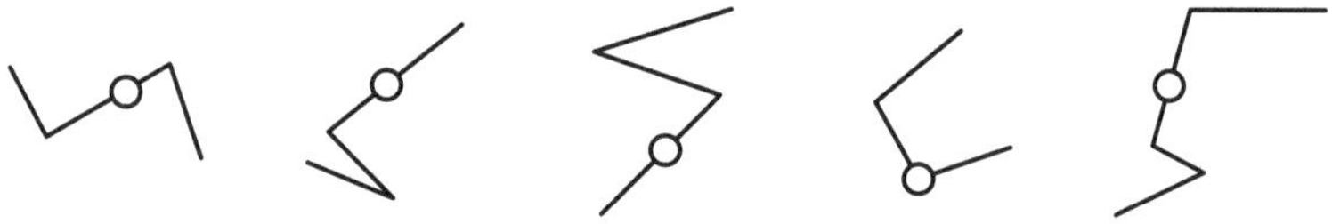

a b c d e

5

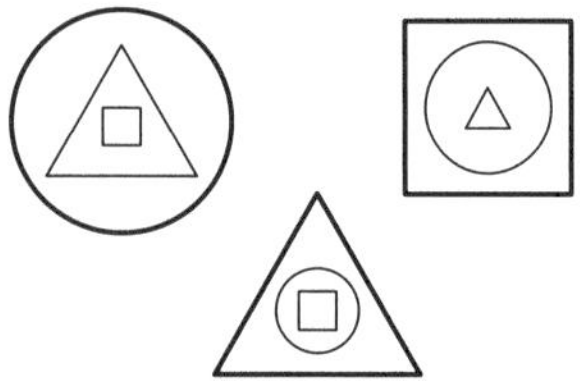

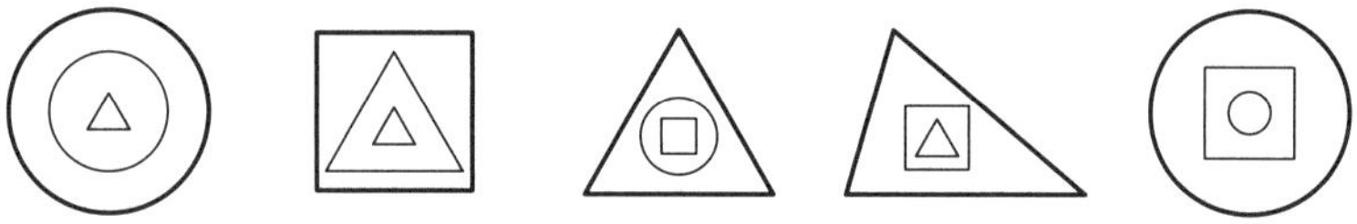

a b c d e

Which one completes the second pair in the same way as the first pair?
Circle the letter.

Example

 is to as is to

a b c d (e)

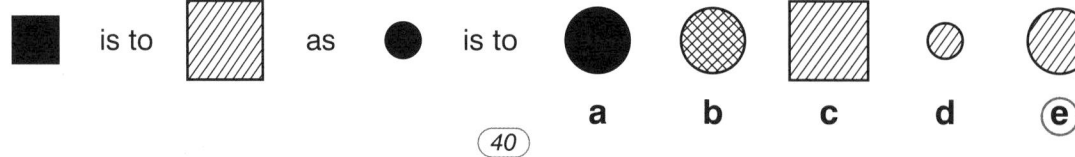

6 is to as is to

a **b** **c** **d** **e**

7 is to as is to

a **b** **c** **d** **e**

8 is to as is to

a **b** **c** **d** **e**

9 is to as is to

a **b** **c** **d** **e**

10 is to as is to

a **b** **c** **d** **e**

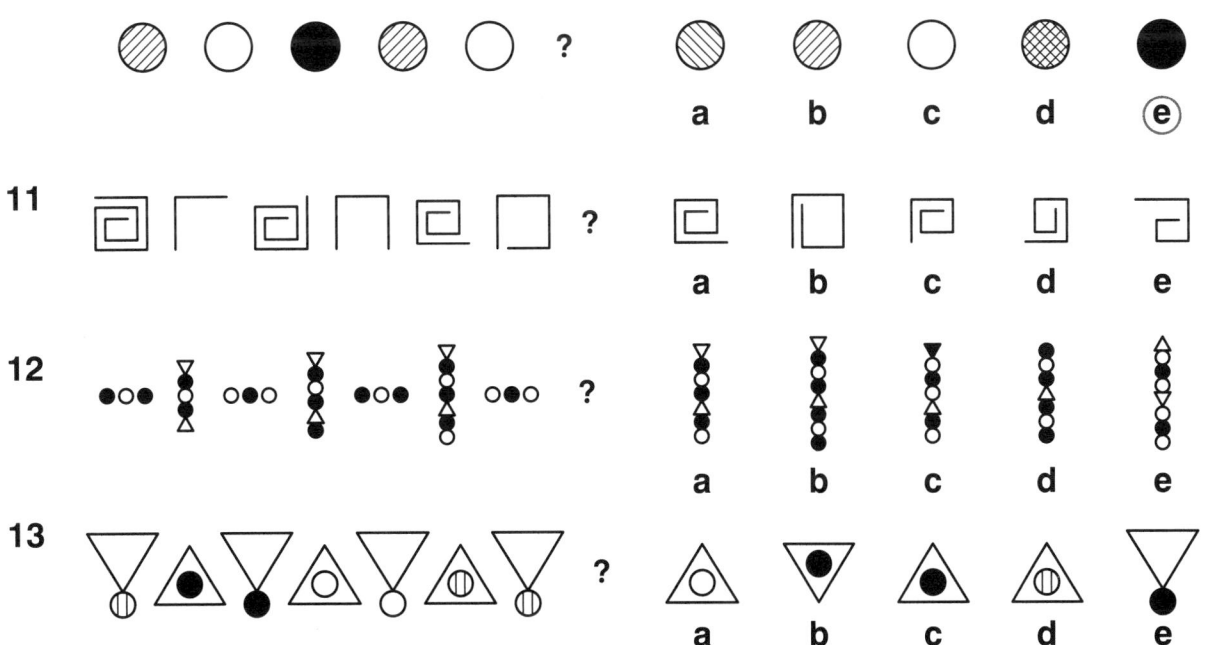

Which one completes the sequence? Circle the letter.

Example

a **b** **c** **d** **e**

11

a **b** **c** **d** **e**

12

a **b** **c** **d** **e**

13

a **b** **c** **d** **e**

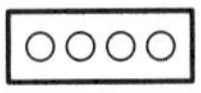

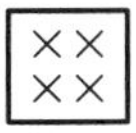

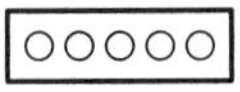

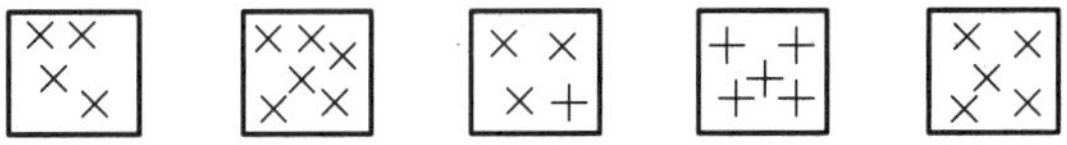

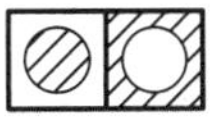

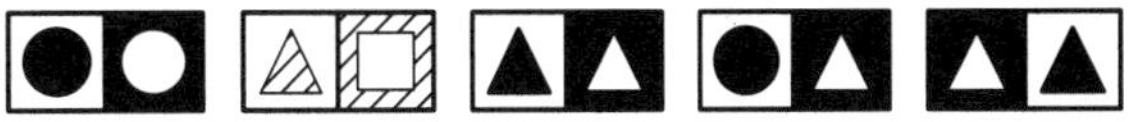

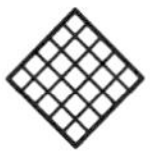

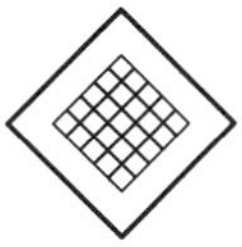

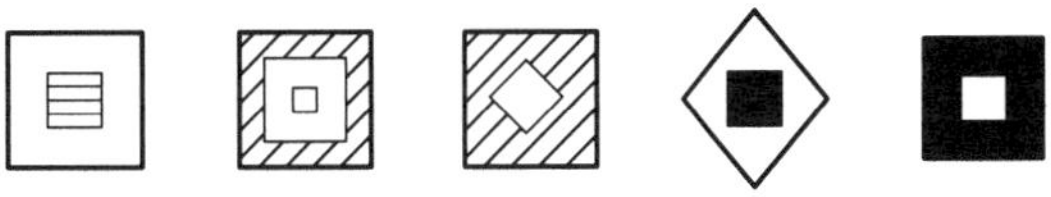

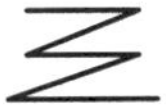

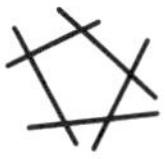

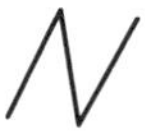

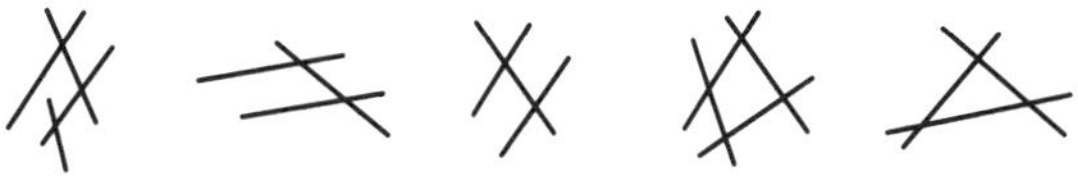

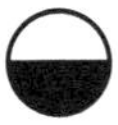

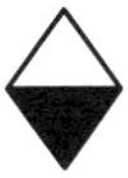

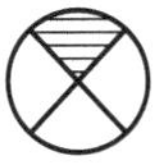

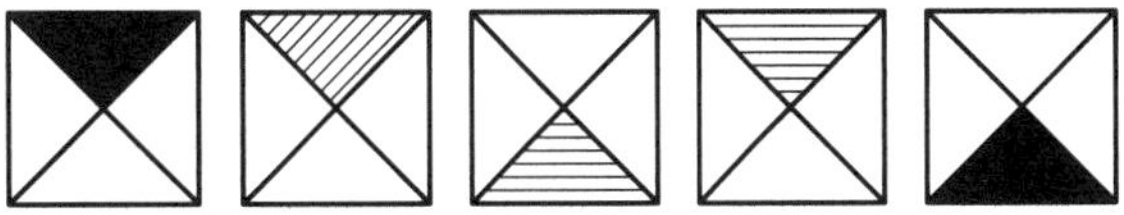

14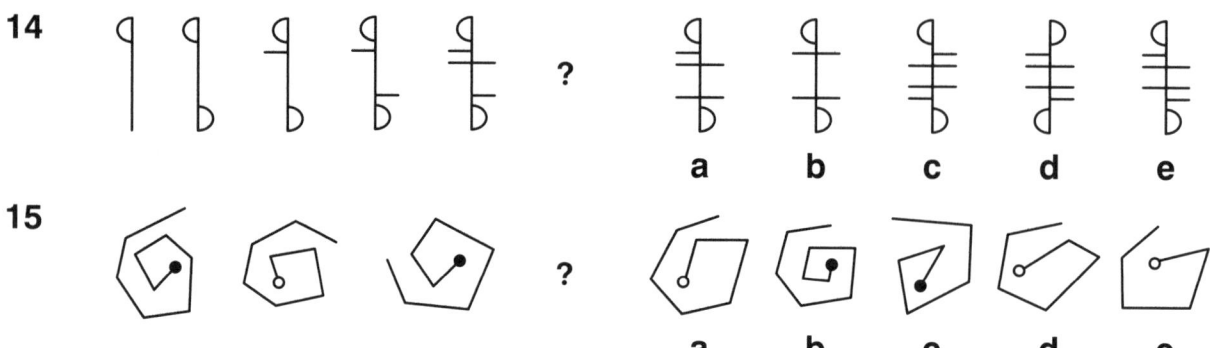

15

Which code matches the last shape? Circle the letter.

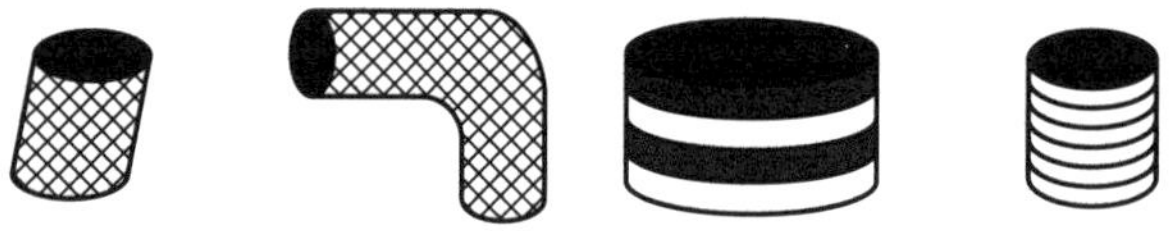

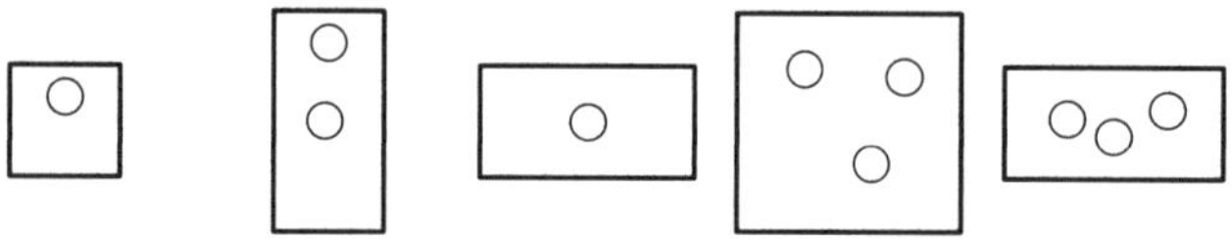

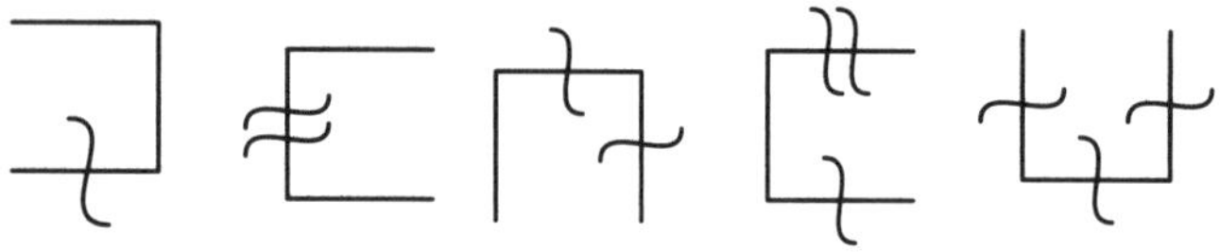

Example

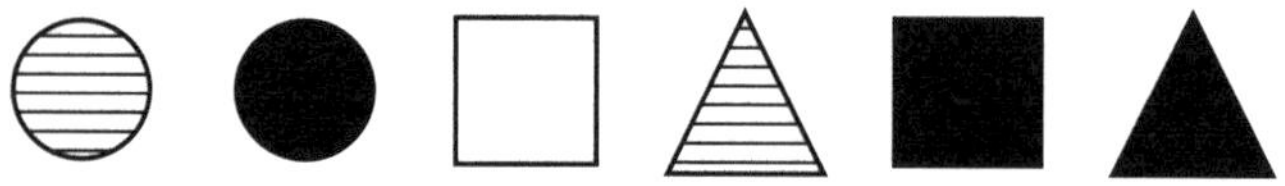

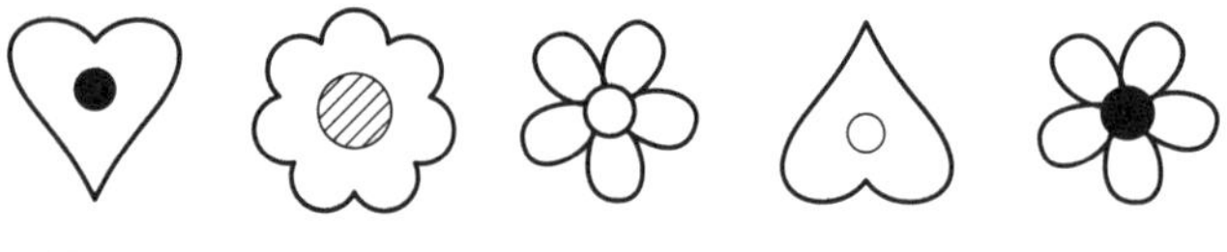

16

17

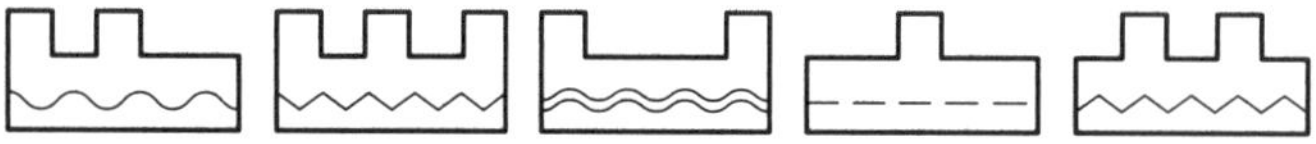

18

19

20

Which one is a reflection of the pattern on the left? Circle the letter.

Example

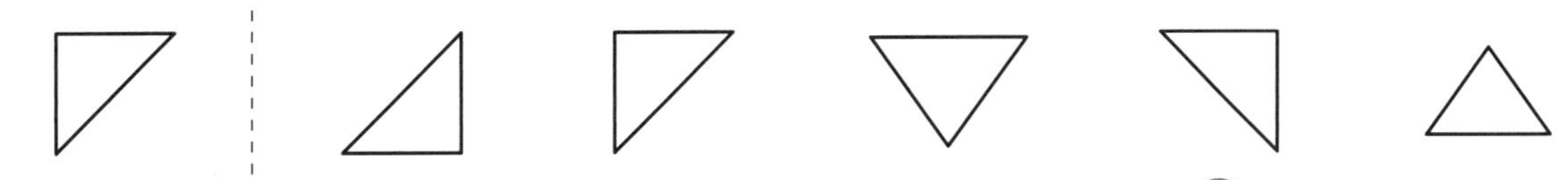

a b c (d) e

21

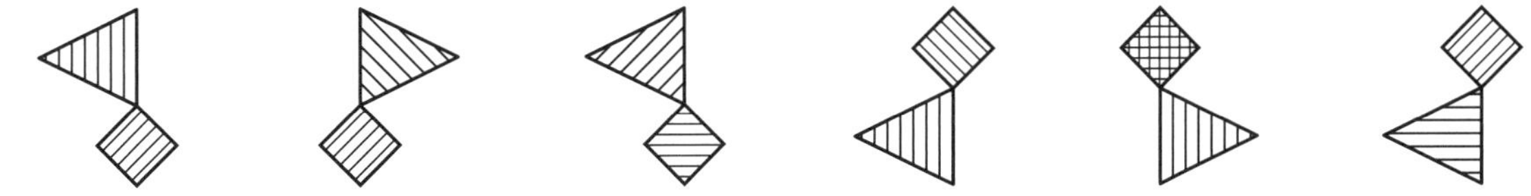

a b c d e

22

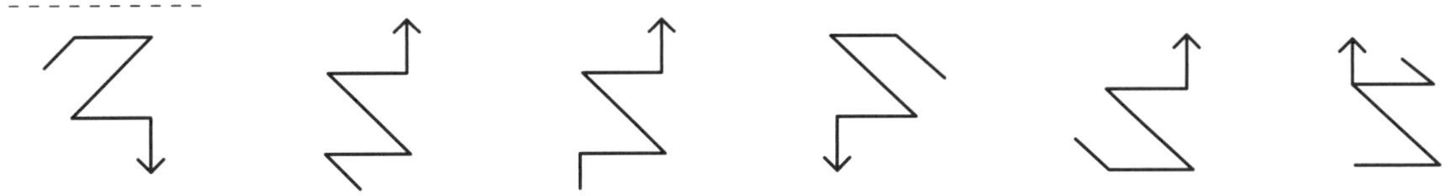

a b c d e

23

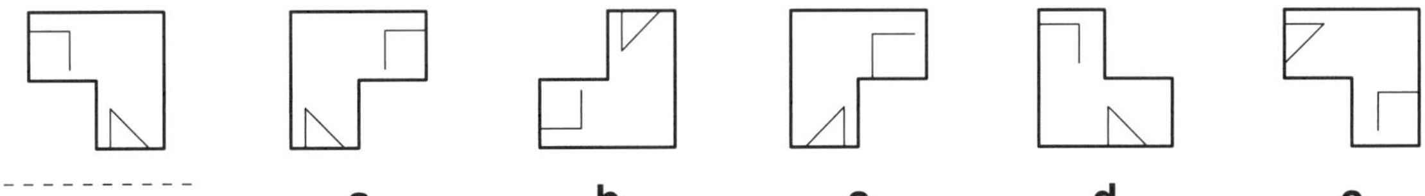

a b c d e

24

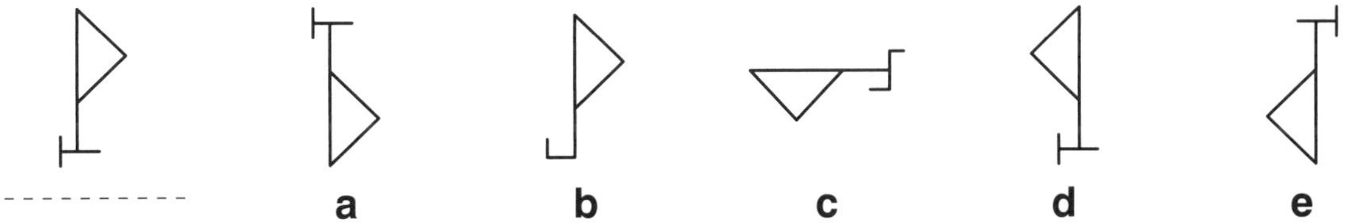

a b c d e

Which one completes the grid? Circle the letter.

Example

a b (c) d e

25

a b c d e

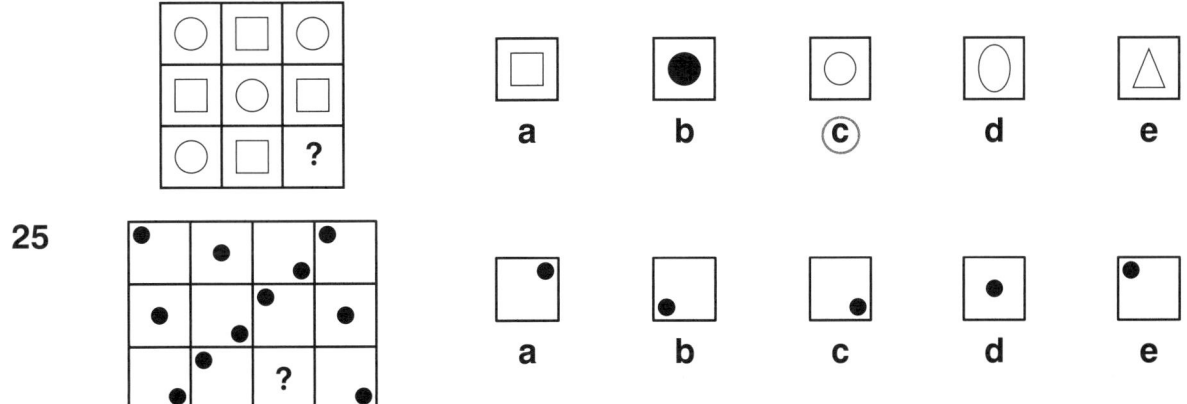

26

27

28

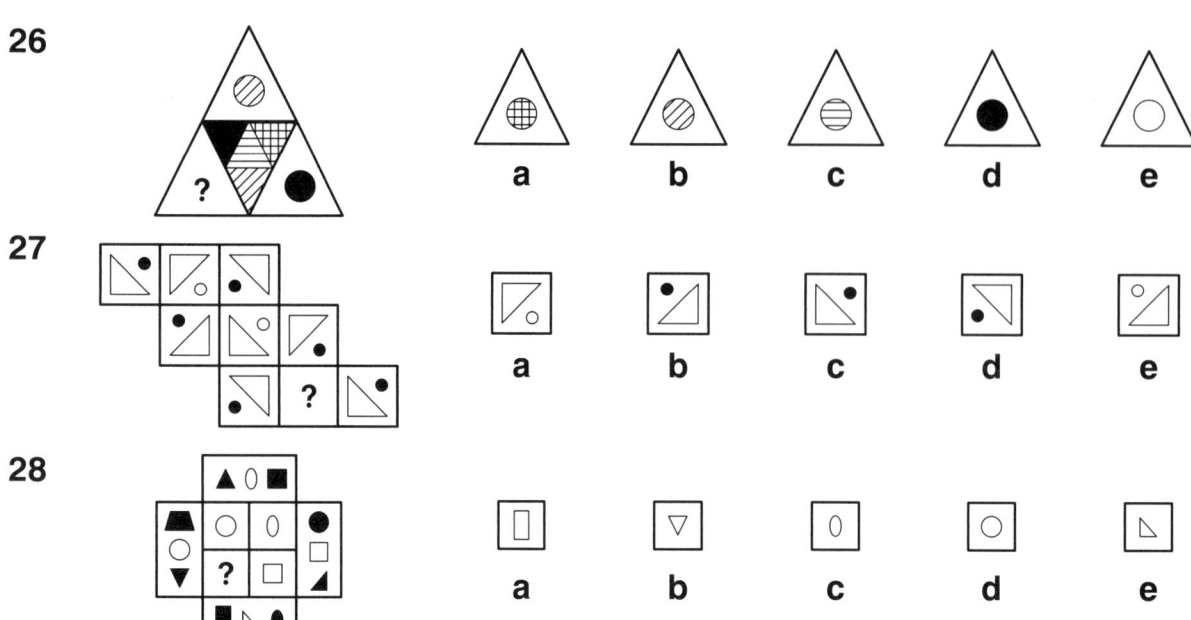

Which of these nets will fold to give the cube on the left? Circle the letter.

Example

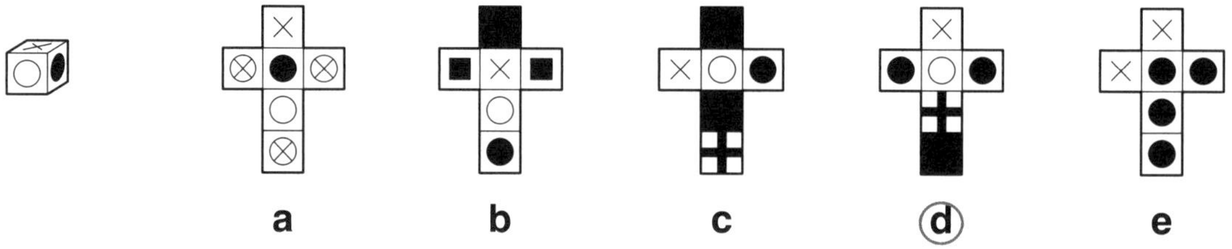

29

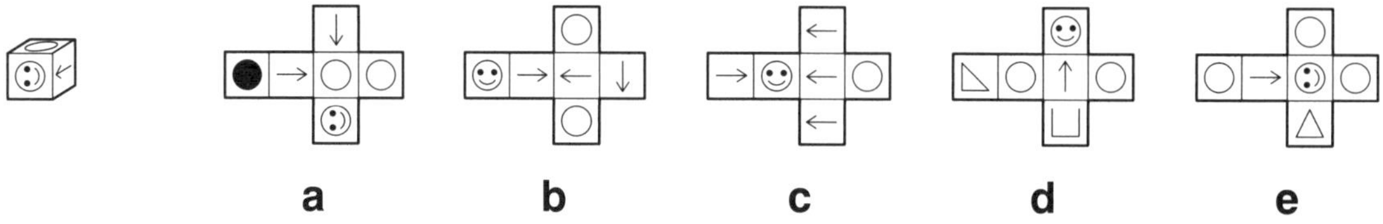

30

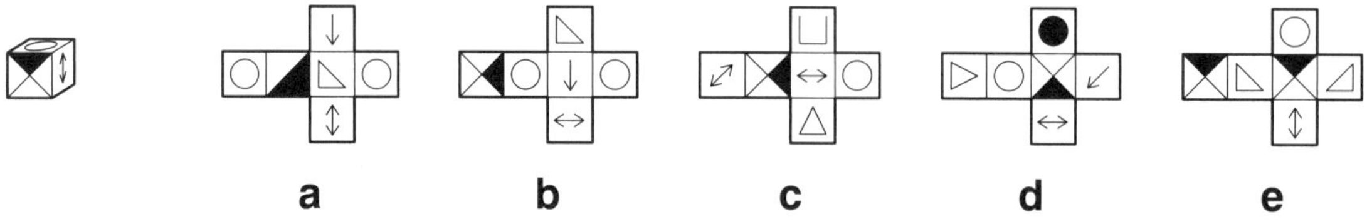

31

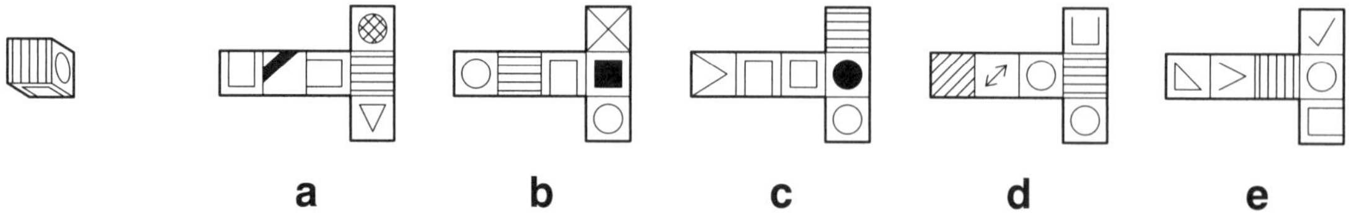

32

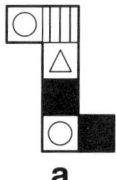

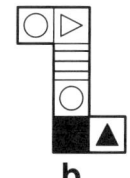

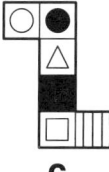

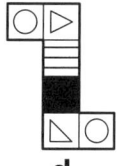

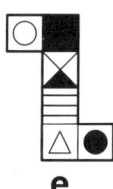

a b c d e

Which pattern is made by combining the two shapes on the left? Circle the letter.

Example

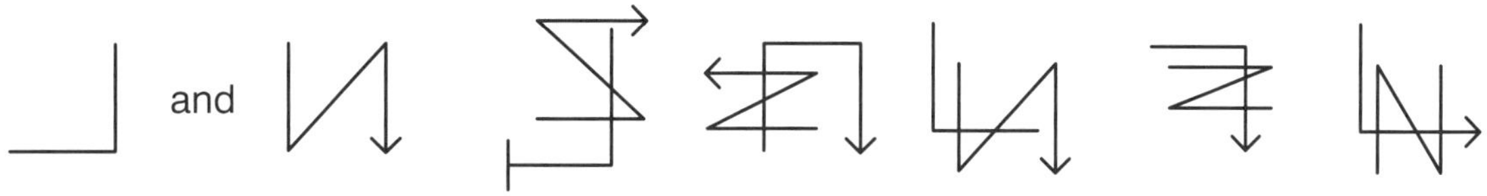

a b (c) d e

33

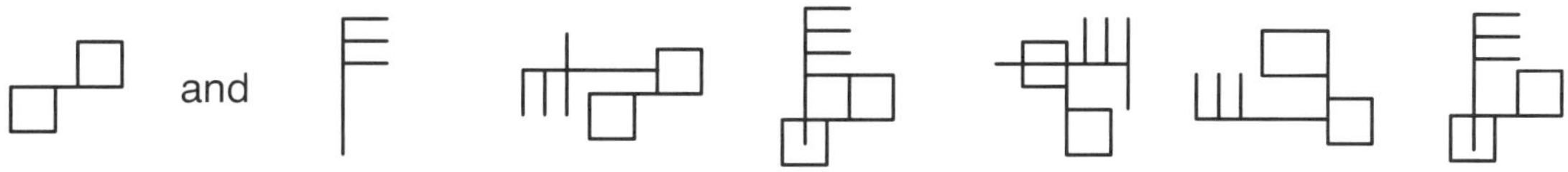

a b c d e

34

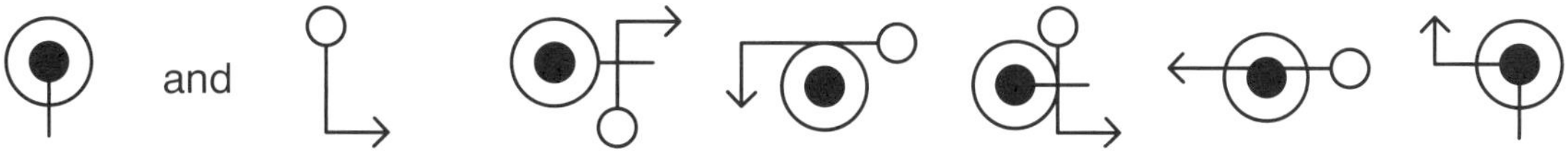

a b c d e

35

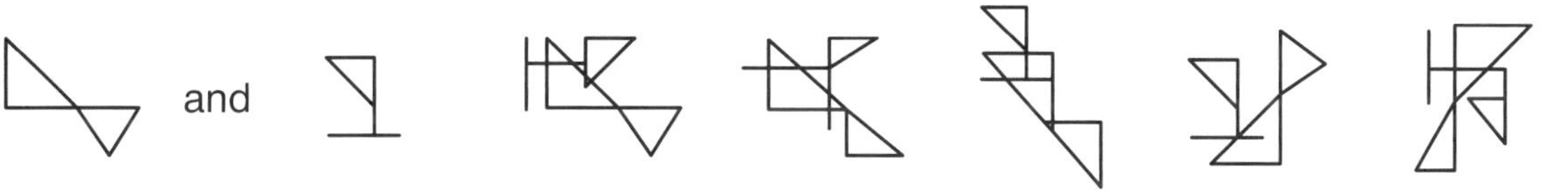

a b c d e

36

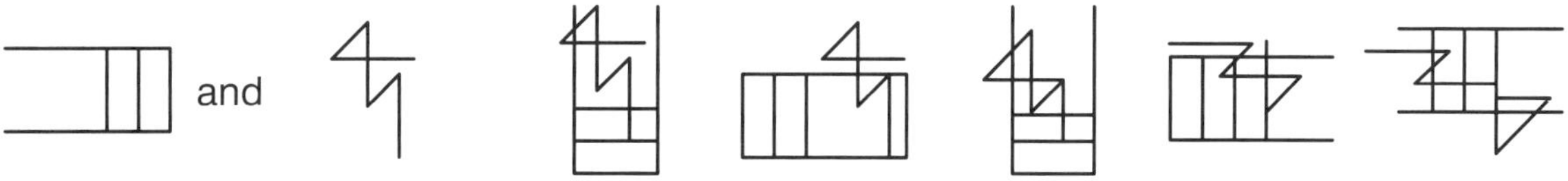

a b c d e

Mixed paper 3

Which one belongs to the group on the left? Circle the letter.

Example

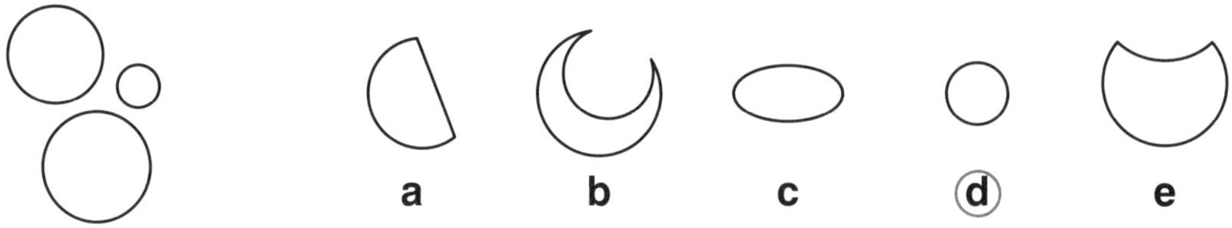

a b c (d) e

1

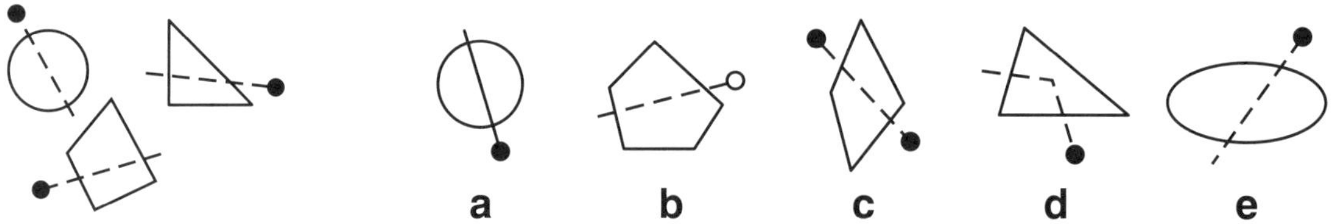

a b c d e

2

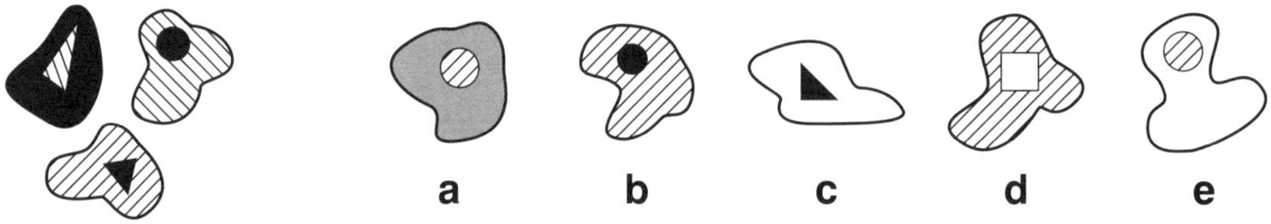

a b c d e

3

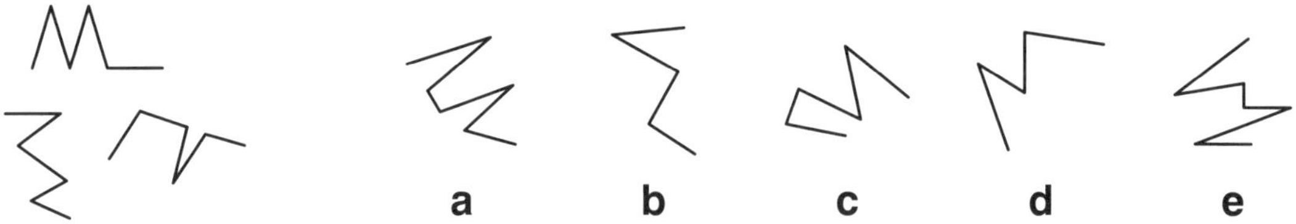

a b c d e

4

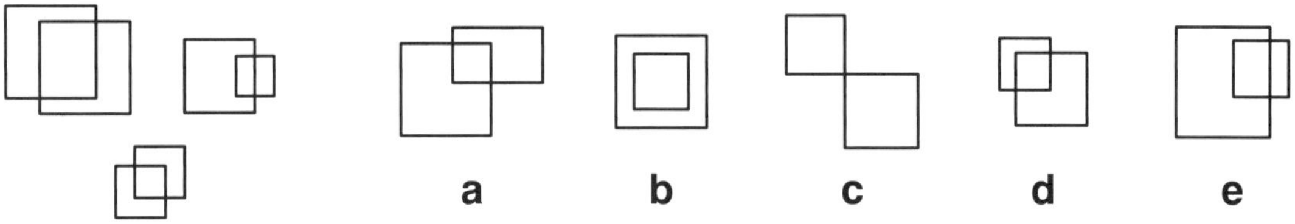

a b c d e

5

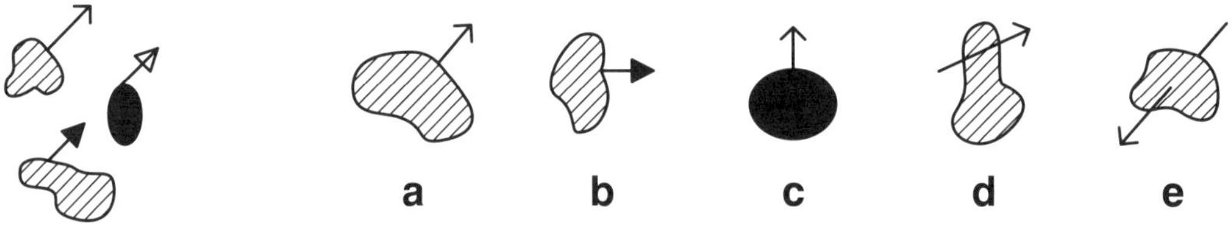

a b c d e

Which one completes the second pair in the same way as the first pair?
Circle the letter.

Example

a b c d (e)

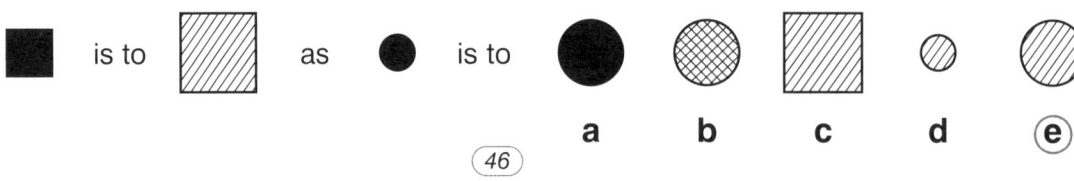

6

7

8

9

10

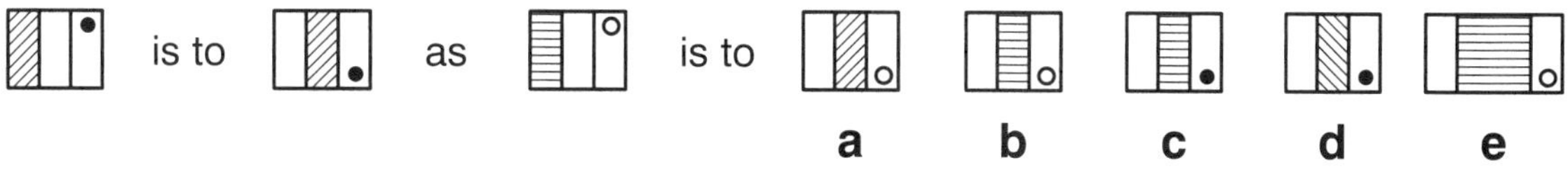

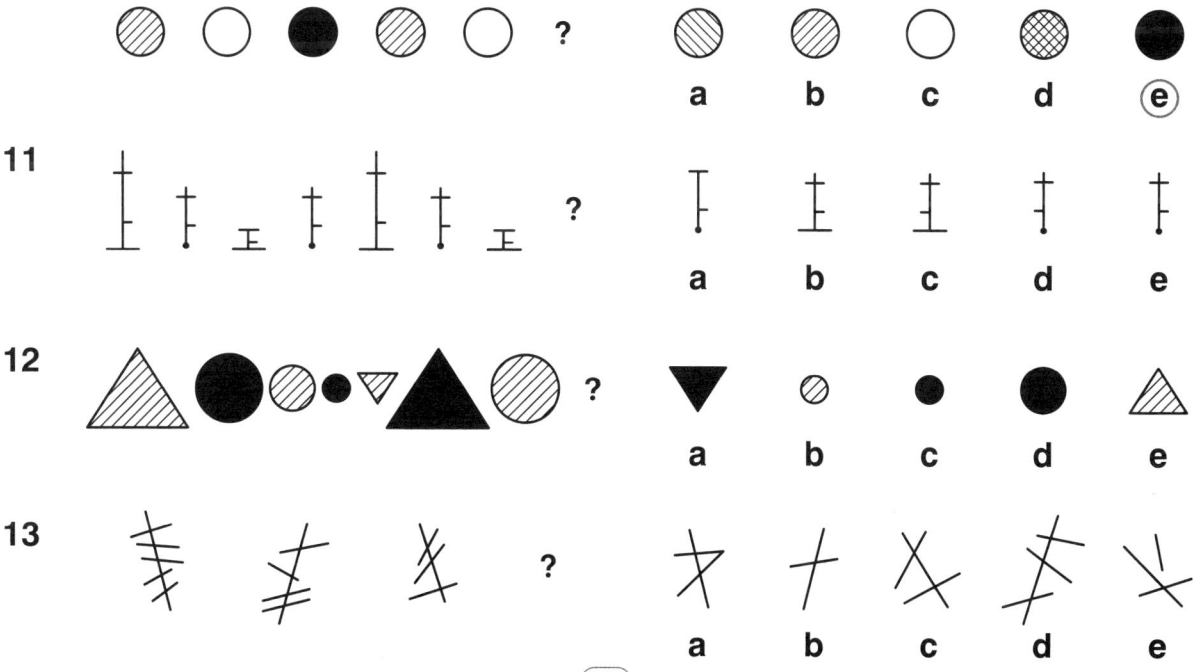

Which one completes the sequence? Circle the letter.

Example

11

12

13

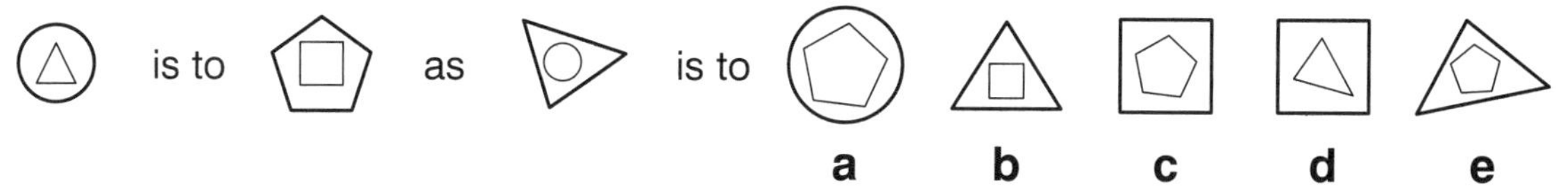

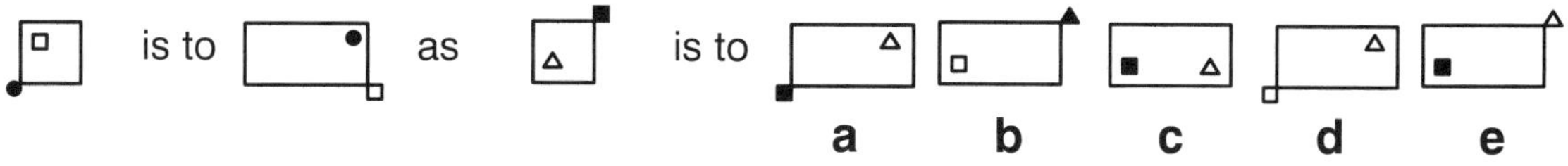

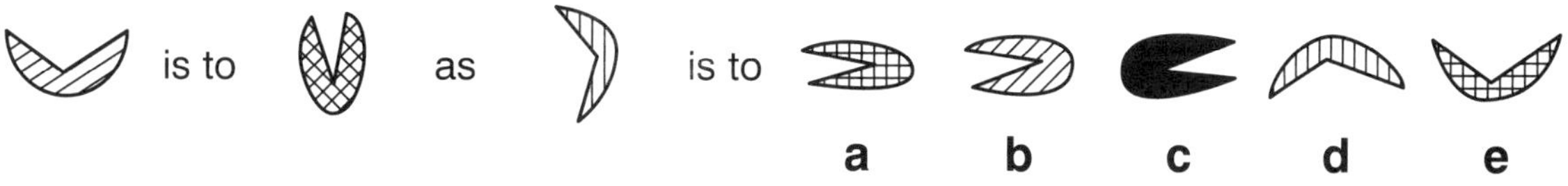

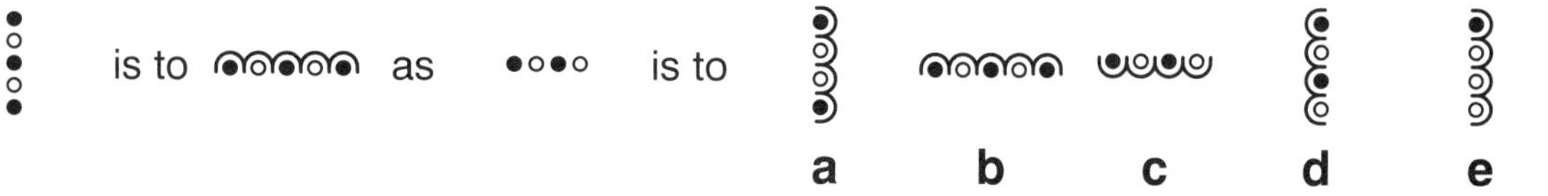

14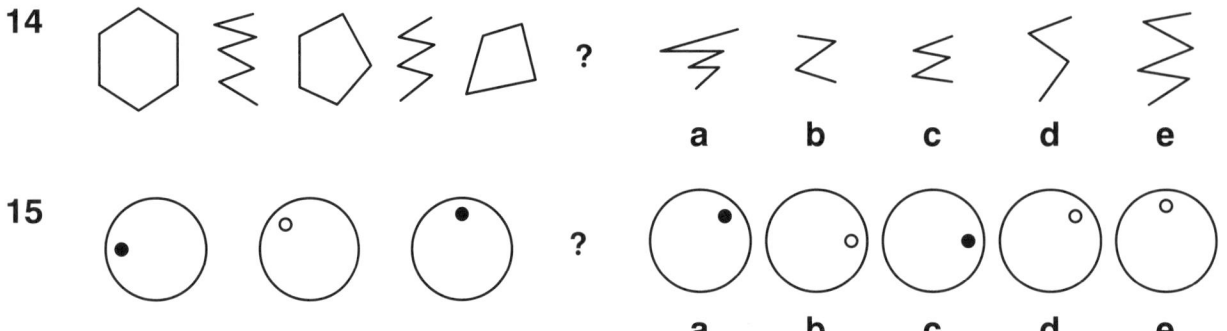

a b c d e

15

a b c d e

Which code matches the last shape? Circle the letter.

Example

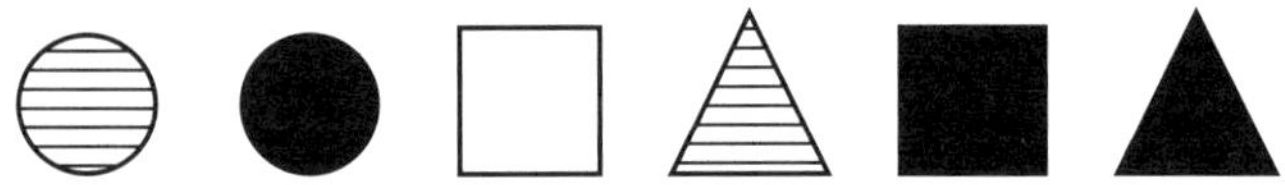

AX BX CY AZ BY ?

AY CX BZ CZ AZ
a b ⓒ d e

16

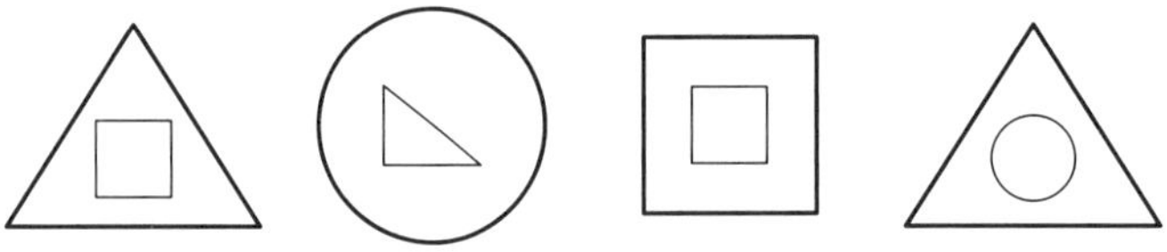

AX BY CX ?

AY CZ AZ CY BZ
a b c d e

17

AX BY CZ CX ?

AZ BZ AY CY BX
a b c d e

18

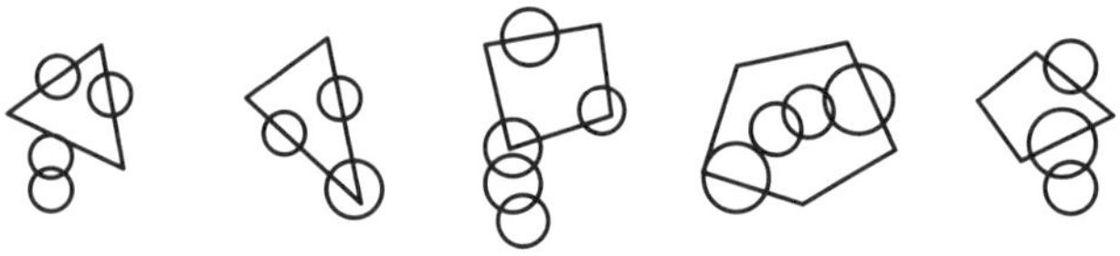

BX AX CY BZ ?

AZ BY CZ CX AY
a b c d e

19

AP BP CQ DR ?

DQ BS CP AS BR
a b c d e

20

FX EZ FY DX ?

EX DY FZ EY DZ
a b c d e

Which one is a reflection of the pattern on the left? Circle the letter.

Example

21

22

23

24

Which one completes the grid? Circle the letter.

Example

25

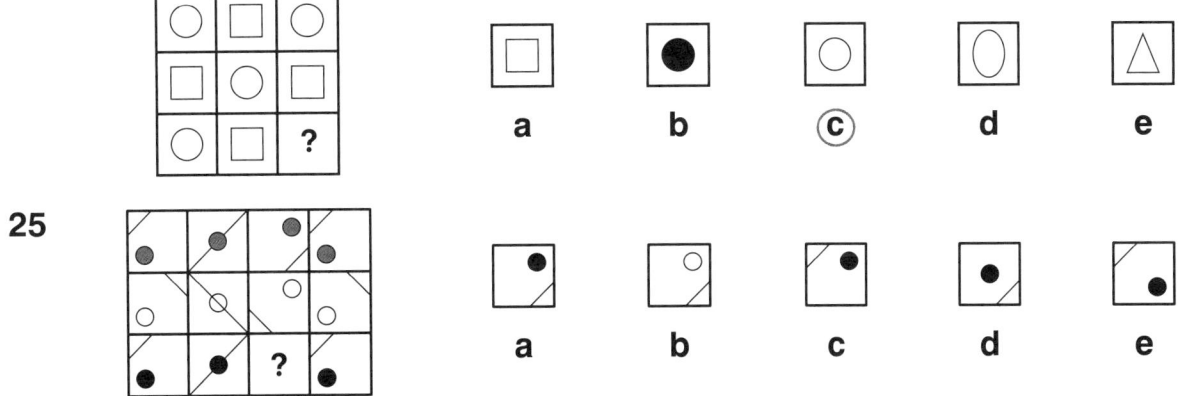

26

27

28

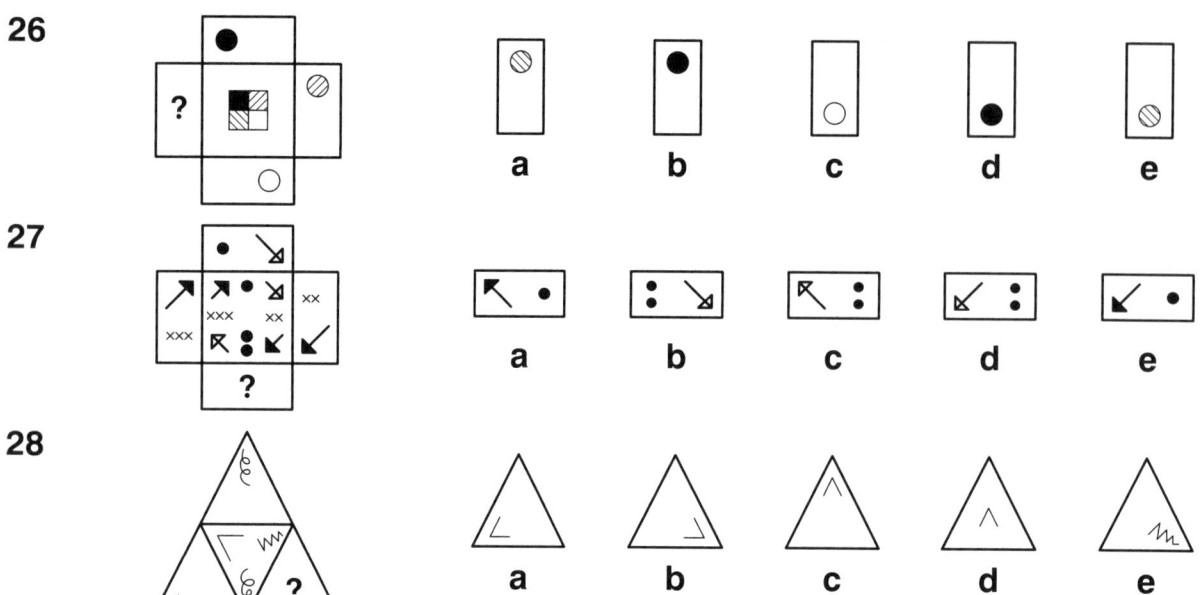

Which of these nets will fold to give the cube on the left? Circle the letter.
Example

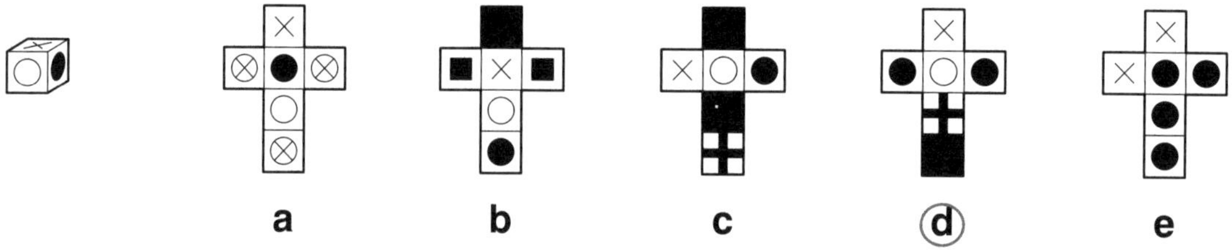

29

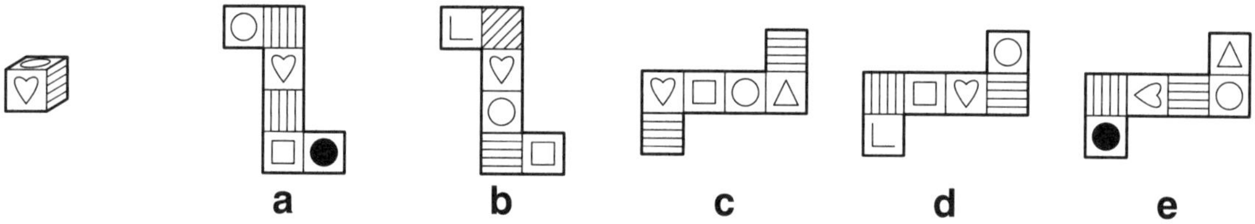

30

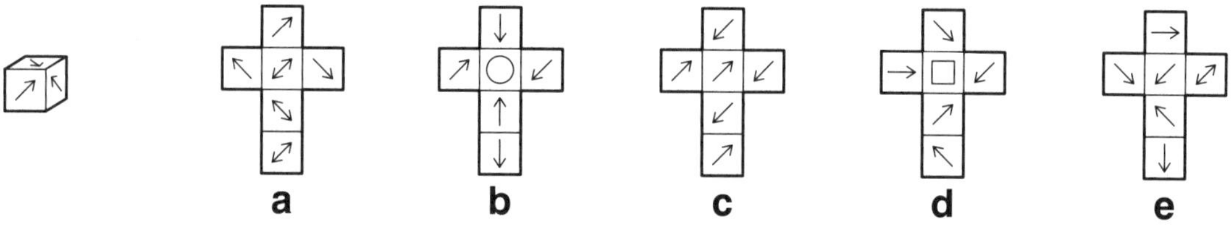

31

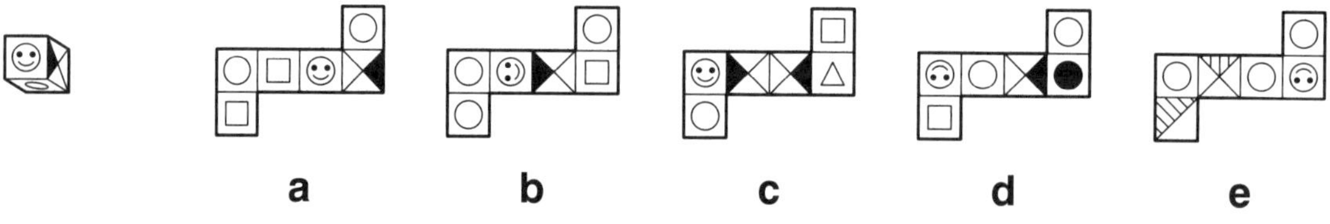

32

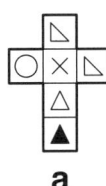

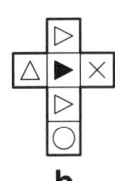

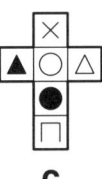

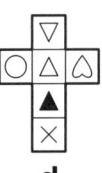

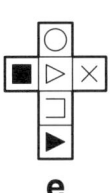

a b c d e

Which pattern is made by combining the two shapes on the left?
Circle the letter.

Example

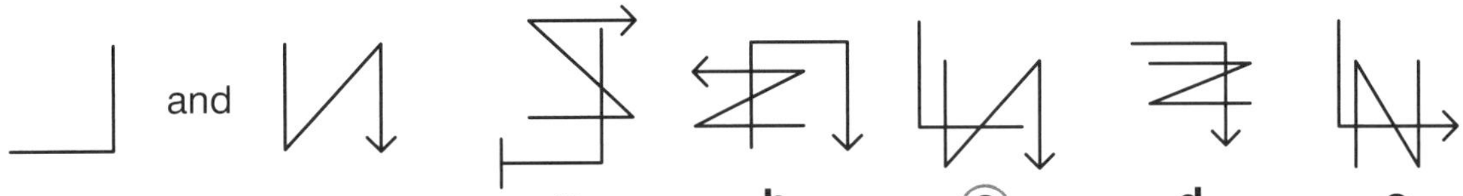

a b (c) d e

33

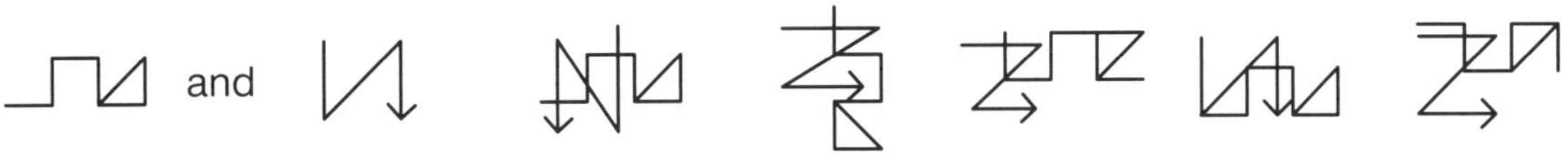

a b c d e

34

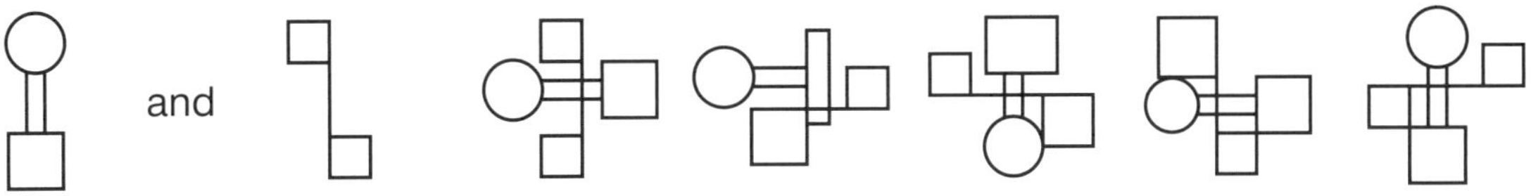

a b c d e

35

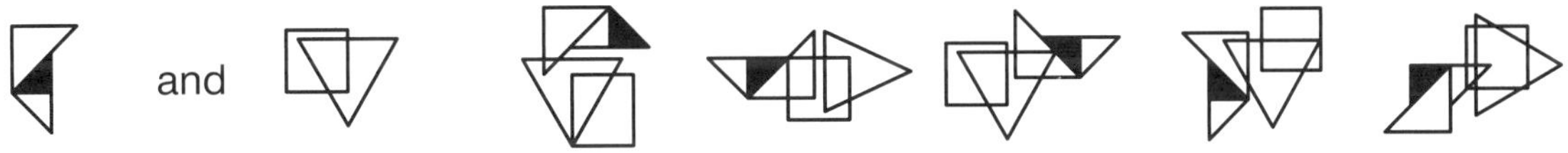

a b c d e

36

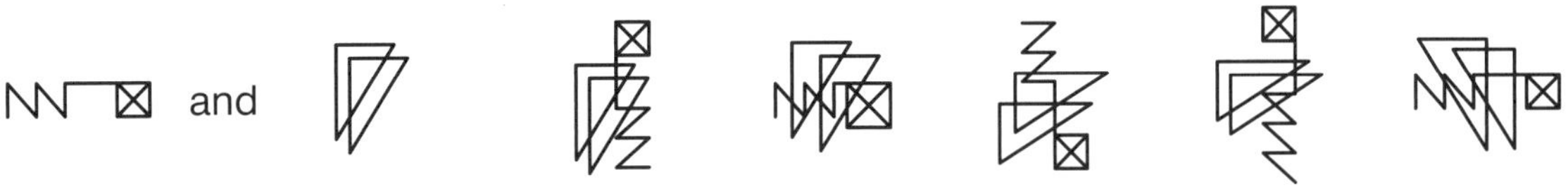

a b c d e